"In a practical way, *Coffee Talks With Messiah* made me want to spend my 'tea times' with Jesus, and this book demonstrated how to do it.

"The section of your book on sexual testing brought about an immediate deliverance for me from an evil counterfeit in this area of my life. The manifestation I thought was from the Lord, was not from the Lord, and reading your experience gave me discernment, and I have renounced it. Now I have reached a higher level of purity in my Christian walk, and being free of this secret deception feels wonderful!"

—S.P.

"Jill Shannon has shared her transparent and teachable spirit so that the very heart of the Father is evident and woven throughout this beautiful tapestry of *Coffee Talks With Messiah*.

"As I have read this book over and over again, I am always refreshed by the relevant and fresh revelation throughout the book. It is grounded in Scripture, with practical guidance for healing to those who are hurting, and a clear testimony for salvation to those who seek Him. I believe this dear and precious sister has purchased gold refined in the fire to share as invaluable preparation for His Bride and very serious training for the Church. This book has made an eternal and indelible mark on my heart and life which has deeply enriched my walk and talk with Yeshua."

—*Cathy Minnick*

"Finally! A book that provokes every part of your being to yearn for more of Jesus. I could not put this book down. I became increasingly jealous for my own intimate relationship with Messiah as Jill humbly shares her testimony and relationship with Him. Jill is a faithful disciple of Yeshua: open, honest, obedient. If you desire true intimacy with Jesus but aren't sure how to achieve this, start reading this book today."

—*Tanya Newman*

Coffee Talks
WITH
MESSIAH

WHEN INTIMACY MEETS REVELATION

Jill Shannon

Gazelle
PRESS

Mobile, AL

ISBN 978-1-58169-250-1
For Worldwide Distribution
Printed in the U.S.A.

Gazelle Press
P.O. Box 191540 • Mobile, AL 36619
800-367-8203

Photograph on page 97: Cathy Minnick
Photographic Artist: Juli Stoltzfus, Impressions Media Design
www.ImpressionsMediaDesign.com
Author photo (back cover): Celebrity Kids, Montgomeryville, PA

TABLE OF CONTENTS

ACKNOWLEDGMENTS

I offer heartfelt gratitude to the Lord Jesus for initiating the writing of this book. He provided me with such astonishing, tangible help from the first words to the breathtaking pace of publication, that I can only marvel at His reality and love.

Thank you to my awesome family for their excellent support and generosity with my time: Dror, Larry, Raviv and Amber, Keren and Ariela, I love you all so much!

There are no words that can express my love and appreciation to my precious friend, Cathy Minnick, who read every word as it came out, edited, prayed, supported and encouraged beyond my wildest imagination. Incredibly, she made my path effortless and joyful. I bless my dearest friends and fellow-intercessors, Dave and Vicki, Theresa and Linda; all of my praying brothers and sisters at Spring City Fellowship, who have been so patient with my many words; and our awesome Pastors John and Sandra Shantz, whose transparent lives and hearts are indescribably generous. I have been utterly vulnerable to these beloved friends, and they have been worthy of my trust. I thank my most loyal friends: Lyn, Amy and Cindy, who rescued and encouraged me during times of mental torment and physical anguish. I would not be who I have become without their love.

I also thank and bless Pastors Curt and Anita Malizzi and the precious prayer warriors at Hopewell Christian Fellowship, for their fellowship and generosity to me. I am in awe of their humility and tireless work on behalf of the flock.

My thanks to my friends and editors, Sandy Plummer, who bravely removed dozens of unnecessary commas, and Pat Myers, who has loved me through the worst times, and offered me wisdom and insight into the reader's heart. I am so grateful to Keith Carroll for his focused and insightful improvements to this book, as well as his kindness and respect. He helped me to enter and navigate the world of publishing, which was wholly unknown to me, and I bless him for his friendship. My thanks to Brian, Kathy and Jeff Banashak at Gazelle Press for their support and dedication to the Lord's work. I appreciate their high standards, integrity and professional quality. Thanks for the hospitality in beautiful Mobile, Alabama.

The following teachers and ministries have enlarged my heart of understanding more than I can express: Sid Roth, Choo Thomas, Dr. Bill Hamon, Robert Stearns, Lance Lambert, Nita Johnson, Carol Levergood, Paul Keith Davis, Dan Juster, Rick Joyner, Mike Bickle, Sadhu Sundar Selvaraj, Lars Enarson, Paul Wilbur, and David Dolan.

To my highly anointed brothers in the Lord, whom I am honored to call friends: David, Brother Chris, Mark and Benjamin, you are golden vessels of honor, hidden in the furnace for such a time as this. Since the Lord has placed you in my life, I know that I am greatly favored!

I honor the memory and heritage of my parents, Irv and Mitzi Sher, who gave me their very best. I miss you guys!

I praise You, Lord God of Abraham, Isaac and Jacob. I would not wish to live one more day without Your unfailing love.

FOREWORD

The biblical truths contained in *Coffee Talks With Messiah* are foundational to this compelling testimony of a Spirit-filled Jewish believer in Jesus.

As God begins to reveal His glory to Jill, she learns a tragic aspect of His perspective on the professing church: many believers sing worship to the Lord, and pray for Him to visit us, but they don't really want the awesome, uncomfortable, and even frightening manifestation of the glory of the God of Abraham, Isaac and Jacob.

This unsettling revelation puts the reader on a journey, even a fast-track to intimacy, transparency and revelatory friendship with the Lord Jesus the Messiah. This intimate friendship with the Lord is surely *not* reserved for the prophets only. It is for every child of God who is desperate for His real and manifest presence. Jill's humble and transparent testimony shows us how available and accessible this kind of walk with the Lord really is, and how freely and joyfully He grants this to all who ask.

In several of these startling experiences, we are confronted with some counterfeit manifestations which are not of the Lord; however, God can permit the enemy to test us for our discernment, growth and critical training in spiritual warfare. Jill has courageously shared and taught on these uncomfortable realities, which few are willing to divulge in a public forum. The purpose for exposing these deceptions is for His children to discern between the authentic manifestations of God's Spirit and the counterfeits of the enemy, who can also display supernatural power.

In the comprehensive biblical teachings layered throughout *Coffee Talks With Messiah,* Jill lays the needed foundation for the next great move of God's Spirit: One New Man, as taught in Ephesians, chapters 2 and 3, as well as in Romans 11. The teachings found in the final chapters of this book supply the scriptural framework for this urgent, end-times revelation of the purposes of God for the salvation of millions of souls upon the earth. We are given the keys to understanding the Lord's desired relationship between the Church and the Jewish people, and His sovereign plans for the enormous last days' harvest of both Jew and Gentile.

I believe that *Coffee Talks With Messiah* is far more than a "cup of coffee." It is a rich and diverse banquet of biblically solid revelations, which will accelerate your intimacy with the Lord. It will dramatically open your heart to His unfailing love for you personally, and His unchanging redemptive purposes for His Church and His beloved Jewish people.

Sid Roth
President, Messianic Vision

INTRODUCTION

This book is my true testimony. Although it contains revelation, I do not consider myself a prophet. I am a Jewish believer in the Messiah Jesus, and I teach the Bible. However, John's Gospel tells us that "His sheep know His voice." Paul asserts in Corinthians, "You can all prophesy in turn, so that everyone may be instructed and encouraged." The prophet Joel predicts: "And I will pour out My Spirit on all flesh...and your sons and daughters will prophesy."

Many books which contain revelatory material have been written by highly prophetic individuals. Having read and enjoyed quite a few of these awesome books, I've noticed that "ordinary" believers can feel that such experiences are far beyond them. Indeed, this perception is sometimes accurate.

I believe this book will greatly encourage the majority of readers who are "just like me." I have never seen the Lord with my eyes open, as one would see a physical person. In my thirty-three years as a believer, I have only had one "open vision" where I saw a scene with my eyes open. This occurred in the early 1980s, and I will document it in the first chapter. I have only heard the audible voice of the Lord once, and this consisted of literally one word, spoken recently when I was in physical distress.

When I use the term "visitation," I am normally not referring to a physical visit of the Lord Jesus in a visible or audible form. I am describing a tangible manifestation of His power, presence and glory which cannot be imagined or created by human desire. These visitations might include visions of Him or other scenarios; these take place with my eyes closed, and the visual image is impressed on my mind and spirit. At other times, visitations might include words of knowledge or revelation; the words are imprinted in my mind, not in my ears. However, in the visitation described in Chapter Three, I experienced something of a higher level which I'm still not sure how to define; the testimony will speak for itself.

As with all extra-biblical prophetic words, I fully understand that the accuracy and reliability of these words are not to be compared with the trustworthiness and authority of the Scriptures, which are my sole foundation for objective truth. All words must be tested by Scripture for content and character.

Throughout the book I call the Lord, "Yeshua." This was the name His parents gave Him, in obedience to the angel who announced His conception. He was called by this name when He walked on earth, and it is the Hebrew word for "Salvation." Because I call the Lord by this name in my private life, I am also calling Him "Yeshua" in my public testimony. He is the Desired of All Nations and will respond to all who call on His name. He is indeed the Lord Jesus Christ and from this point on, I will often refer to His true Hebraic identity.

The Lord's primary purpose for the writing of this book is to cultivate, enable and accelerate greater personal intimacy with the Lord Yeshua the Messiah;

the astonishing reality of this intimacy is available to each one who seeks Him earnestly. Intimacy is a two-way relationship. It is vital for every believer to know Him through His Word, but the other half of the relationship consists of the Lord knowing us.

Did you ever wonder how the Lord could say to professing Christians, "I never knew you"? The Lord knows everything, including all the thoughts of our hearts. How could He say He doesn't know us? The Lord Yeshua desires that every believer will understand the critical difference between His omniscience and the voluntary transparency of His children's hearts. The testimony of my book is the unfolding of this rarely-taught lesson, one that has changed my life with Him forever. The following Scriptures are so chilling that we would do anything to avoid hearing these irrevocable words spoken to us on the last day:

> *But while they* [the five foolish virgins] *were on their way to buy the oil, the bridegroom arrived. The virgins who were ready went in with him to the wedding banquet. And the door was shut. Later the others also came. "Sir! Sir!" they said. "Open the door for us!" But he replied, "I tell you the truth, I don't know you"* (Matt. 25:10-12).

> *Many will say to me on that day, "Lord, Lord, did we not prophesy in your name, and in your name drive out demons and perform many miracles?" Then I will tell them plainly, "I never knew you. Away from me, you evildoers!"* (Matt. 7:22-23)

The Lord tells us that not only do His sheep know Him, but that He knows them as well (John 10:14, 27). The apostle Paul describes the difference between knowing and being known in this way: "The man who thinks he knows something does not yet know as he ought to know. But the man who loves God is known by God" (1 Co. 8:2-3).

Although I was a believer for more than thirty years, I did not understand the Lord's love for me or His eagerness to hear everything that was in my heart. My walk and intimacy with the Lord Yeshua are transparent in this book; so are the mistakes, sins and flawed ways of thinking which have been a part of my journey and process.

If I am privileged to teach others about intimacy, I am required to reveal the way I live, think and speak with the Lord in all sorts of situations. In order to demonstrate my vulnerability and transparency with the Lord, I must display this same vulnerability to the reader. I pray that you will be as patient and charitable towards me in your hearts as is our most gentle and humble King.

As you read, may you be excited and encouraged in your intimate walk with Him; may you be enlarged in your love and devotion to the dearest and most faithful Savior a broken and fallen person could ever hope to find. My love goes out to everyone who reads this book. May He add His Spirit of confirmation to these written words so that they might be found to be faithful and true.

PART I

KNOWING GOD

CHAPTER 1

RELIGION WITHOUT RELATIONSHIP

In the beginning, all the days of my life were written in Your Book. Before I was conceived, You knew who I would become. You knew the radiant little girl with a sensitive spirit; the depressed Jewish adolescent; the corporate instructor; the Israeli mother of toddlers; the pianist and psalmist; and on the day inscribed in Your Book, the resolute servant who would...but I get ahead of myself.

Mitzi was in advanced labor as she drove herself to Mt. Sinai Hospital on the Upper East Side of Manhattan. She parked on the street and walked several blocks into the delivery room. It was three o'clock on a May afternoon and Eisenhower was president. My father Irv was pursuing his doctorate in biochemistry and met my mother at the hospital to support her and photograph the birth. The doctor was home in time for supper that evening.

My parents were pleased and proud of such a beautiful first child, a daughter they named Jill. Despite tradition, they decided not to name me after a departed relative. Photographs would be abundant from that day forward.

The excitement and delight of new parents provide a comforting experience for a baby, and this security extends into the childhood years. I am grateful for all the love and benefits that my dear Mitzi and Irv bestowed on me consistently, even into the last difficult years of our time together. I honor their memories and those of my adoring grandparents as well.

Even so, there is a deeper sense of acceptance into this world that I did not receive from my parents, which was the welcome of the One who actually created me. My family simply did not know that the God of our ancestors was personally and lovingly involved in the creation of each child born into the world.

As a bright and articulate child, I was inquisitive, contented and pleasing to all adults in my sphere; yet from my earliest memories, I experienced an inward sense of "unwelcome" or an unworthiness to exist on this earth. It grew into a sense of inadequacy, performance anxiety and churned into a deep melancholy as the pressures of adolescence developed.

My mother and father were highly educated and operated as enlightened humanists, "good people" by all the normal standards of this world.

Nevertheless, they could not impart the spiritual foundation needed to morally anchor an insecure and restless daughter, one who was rapidly developing a gaping spiritual void they were unable to fill.

I knew from synagogue attendance and years of Hebrew school that God was the "thing" I needed to fill the hole in my constantly aching heart. Although I privately prayed in bed every night and I did believe that He heard me, I did not hear His voice in my heart, nor did I know His character or biblical requirements for His people.

Due to my family's comfortable circumstances and their exceeding generosity to their children, God's blessings in my life were very evident, and I sensed that He loved me. Even so, it could not be said that I had a personal relationship with God, or that I understood the concepts of righteousness, holiness or sin. I wanted a relationship with Him, but could not hear any voice beyond my own thoughts and emotions. I now wonder whether I could have distinguished His voice from my inner confusion, had He been speaking to me during my unhappy adolescent years. Why did my Hebrew school not address this need for relationship? Where was the Reality and Presence of God in our ancient religion?

Transitions and Salvation

My first year away at college was 1973, and it brought the usual temptations for an eighteen-year-old who had been closely sheltered. The primary negative influences to which I was quickly exposed were pot, hashish, radical feminism and a first boyfriend with some unhealthy attitudes. That was tuition well spent! I also attended classes (of all things) and suddenly learned that I actually had to work very hard to attain good grades. After a lifetime of straight A's with minimal effort, this rigorous demand came as a shock to my system. After an overwhelmingly difficult chemistry course, my depression increased; I even entertained thoughts of suicide from time to time.

During the summer after my first year away, I was at home and visiting with my friend, Lyn, whom I had known since junior high. She told me she had "become a Christian." I had always learned that a person was either Jewish or Christian. Everyone who wasn't Jewish was automatically "the other." I explained to Lyn that she had always been a Christian. Then she explained to me that she had come into a "personal relationship with Jesus" that she had never known, despite her Gentile upbringing.

As the summer progressed, I asked her every ponderous question that an unfulfilled yet skeptical college student would ask. All my questions and all her answers could be the subject of another book. (For a fascinating dialogue of tough questions by a skeptic and marvelous answers by Jesus, read *Dinner with a Perfect Stranger.*[1])

Finally, I asked her something about the people in the world who never heard of Jesus, and the potential injustice of God. Oddly, her simple answer ended my month-long interrogation. "Jill, God is just. Jesus is coming back whether you believe it or not."

I was stunned at the simplicity of this statement. His return was an absolute future reality, irrespective and independent of my subjective beliefs. Objective truth was *not* connected to our personal opinions and beliefs! I did not want to be living my present lifestyle when He returned. I already sensed that this event could be a dreadful moment in history.

Interestingly, my Judaism did not seem to be at all contradictory to what I was about to embrace. I knew perfectly well that Yeshua (Jesus) was Jewish. I had learned this in eighth grade while slow-dancing with a cute Italian boy. He whispered in my ear that unlike many Catholics, he liked the Jews. Knowing nothing of anti-Semitism, I listened, naïve and perplexed, as "Cherish" played romantically in the background. He continued, "Anytime my mother hears someone say, 'those dirty Jews,' my mother says, 'Our Lord was a Jew.'"

I pulled back from his overly familiar embrace and stared at him with huge eyes of astonishment and declared, "That's true! She's right!" At age fourteen, I now had a new truth in my heart that would never be far from my thoughts until my last day on earth.

One week before returning to Tufts University, I prayed with Lyn and turned my heart toward Yeshua to receive atonement and forgiveness for my sins. My sinful nature was evident to me, and I now knew that my longstanding sense of guilt and unworthiness was accurate. I had always felt unclean, but no one could help me understand it or rectify this condition. I now realized that Yeshua's sacrifice was the only act of cleansing which could restore me to the accepting and loving relationship with God for which I was created. Our Hebrew Scriptures were full of the sacrifice of animals to restore the worshiper to God, and our father Abraham was asked to sacrifice his only son; why could this sinless man not offer Himself as a perfect sacrifice on our behalf?

I can never express my gratitude to Lyn, who has brought me into an intimate relationship with our most gracious Lord, my own Yeshua! Blessings upon my sister and her family forever and ever! Amen.

His Welcome Into the World

Despite believing in the Lord and serving Him for many years, I continued to carry a weight of unworthiness and self-hatred which I did not know how to address. It was not until the day of my fifty-second birthday, three decades after receiving Yeshua as my Lord, that He addressed the long-standing pain in my heart which had been buried. He sent me His prophetic word concerning the day of my birth and the "unwelcome" undercurrent that I had ignored all of these years.

I have always coped well and performed at a high level without admitting to an internal grief and shame, which cannot be accessed or healed apart from a revelation from our Creator. Here is a portion of the word I received from my dear friend Katya, as she had received it from the Father's heart for my birthday; she also gave me the gift of a little stuffed kitten which was a baby present from Yeshua, welcoming me into this world:

> The great joy of your birth was felt in Me. I welcomed you with wide open arms. You were softer than this very soft little stuffed kitten. I was the proud Papa and Mama who welcomed you into My world. You were birthed from Me before you were birthed by your own flesh and blood mother.
>
> Your parents were proud to have such a beautiful little girl. They were pleased about you, your beauty, and how you would make them proud. They did their very best for you, nothing less for their little princess that they did not know was really a Princess!
>
> I knew you before you entered the womb of the world. I knit you in the dark and secret place. I comforted you in that place. As I guided you down the path to the open, bright and cold place, You did not know MY welcome through your parents.
>
> Today I give you the knowledge, blessing and even the covering of My Welcome which was always there for you, as I stood by the bed when you were handed to your mother, as a newborn baby. My welcome remains warm, true, loving and safe…completely satisfying and real.
>
> I knew how perfectly I had made you already, while your mother and father made sure you had ten fingers and ten toes. I counted them too, just to touch those tiny, silky soft and beautiful, long, slender fingers and toes. Already I wanted to play with you, and counting with them was My way to let you know that your daddy and mama were there for you. I knew those beautiful fingers would bless Me in worship, praise and in the playing of stringed and keyed instruments. I knew before you ever opened your mouth and lungs to cry, that this precious and beautiful mouth and voice would sing more beautifully than the most intricate and beautiful birdsong to Me.
>
> I am restoring the joy, warmth and welcome of birth, motherhood and childhood to you, as you rest in My arms of love, and know My whole and complete love for you.

Despite the kindness of this most intimate word from the Lord, it was not easy for me to believe that God was personally present and rejoiced in the day of my birth. "So many babies are born into the world every day," I reasoned. "How and why would He care about one baby, born in New York City to secular Jewish parents who did not honor Him?" My feelings about this prophetic word exposed the pain and mistrust in my heart, and He taught me more about His love through this word and my initial response to it. He knew us by name before we were conceived. Yet the Bible warns us repeatedly that some professing Christians will hear those chilling words, "I never knew you." Surely, we would pay any price on this earth to ensure that the Lord Jesus will tell us, on that day, that He knew us.

Early Faith and Messianic Judaism

I returned to my second year of college a radically changed person. My lifestyle of freshman year was instantly replaced with one of relative purity and obedience to my own ancient Scriptures, which had never seemed real or relevant to me before. Now they were bursting with fresh truth and guidance for all of my daily choices. I say "relative" purity because I was obviously not perfected in my thoughts and words at the moment of my salvation but continue to purify my heart to this day.

During these years as a new believer on campus, I was greatly helped and befriended by the Tufts Christian Fellowship. This group of dedicated Christian students and an Inter-Varsity leadership team grounded me in my early walk of faith. They taught me essential principles of discipleship and tools for Bible study. I am indebted to these dear friends, who remain in my heart as foundation stones that the Lord used to establish me in Him.

Two years later, I graduated early from Tufts and planned to remain in Boston with my believing friends. But during the Thanksgiving weekend, the Lord kept me up all night, and I asked Him the reason for this restlessness in my spirit through the night hours. I heard His Spirit clearly tell me to move back to my parents' home in Philadelphia, complete my graduate work there, and begin attending a Messianic Jewish congregation.

Up until that night I had only heard of Christian churches and Jewish synagogues. I had no idea that there were already a significant number of Jewish believers in Jesus in my city who worshipped in a Messianic congregation. This is now common knowledge, but in 1975, it was relatively new and certainly unheard of in my sphere. It was at this congregation that I began singing in a Messianic worship group which included performing some of my own songs. It was also here that I met Drew, now my husband.

Drew and I dated for a year, mainly pursuing travel and activities related to the singing group and congregation. We married in 1977 and began our careers at the same corporation. We lived for the first five years as busy young professionals; we attended both a home church and a conservative synagogue, in order to become more familiar with traditional Jewish liturgy.

Vision of Creation

One day in 1981, I was reading my Bible at work. Theoretically, I should not have been doing this during my working hours, but this did not stop the Lord from giving me the only open vision I have ever had.

I was reading Genesis and absorbing the amazing story of Creation. As I read the words, they started to take on a reality I had never perceived before. Suddenly, I was no longer reading but was rather seeing the earth in its first moments or days after Creation! I saw a vista before my eyes that was breathtaking in its pristine rugged beauty. It was a huge landscape of an uninhabited expanse of canyons and rocky hills. The cleanness and virginity of the earth brought tears to my eyes as I realized how we have sullied His creation. The sky was vast, with streaks of orange and pink mingled in with the blue heavens. I sensed it was sunrise. This may have been the period between the fourth and fifth day of creation.

I then felt the words: "Let the waters teem with living creatures…" and I immediately saw deep oceans which had been empty moments before, but now teemed with thousands of fish. They were too varied and numerous to estimate, but they suddenly existed, full of life and swimming vigorously. The water seemed alive with activity, purpose and energy. Then His spoken Word continued, "…and let birds fly above the earth and across the expanse of the sky." I then saw the empty sky become densely populated with thousands of birds, flying, calling to each other, busy and full of life. Their dark silhouettes contrasted with the bright blue and orange firmament. Their excited noises shattered the silence, and I was overjoyed to see the air replete with living creatures. I wept at this unbelievable creativity and beauty, and the vision ended. I later wrote a song about it.

I keep asking that the God of our Lord Jesus Christ, the glorious Father, may give you the Spirit of wisdom and revelation, so that you may know him better (Eph. 1:17).

The Call to Leave

In 1982, I applied for a different kind of position in my company. I prayed that the Lord would grant me this promotion and got myself very worked up about it. When I did not get it, I was surprised and quite disappointed. I went for a walk later that day and poured out my complaint before the Lord.

"I know You could have opened that job to me. You must have had a reason for not giving it to me. What was that reason?"

His most unexpected answer came into my mind immediately and consisted of one word: "*Israel.*"

I was taken aback, but it seemed clear to me what this meant. The Lord had deliberately not granted me a new position which would have required several years for me to feel competent. He wanted us to make "Aliyah" (the Hebrew word for immigration to Israel, literally, "going up" to the Land) and begin a new life there. Nothing in me wanted to leave my home, job, parents, friends and support structures, to go to an unknown situation in Israel. It did not sound exciting or attractive to me in any way. It was a terrifying thought and yet, was it really Him?

I decided not to mention this "revelation," consisting of exactly one word, to my husband. Part of me hoped it would quietly fade into the oblivion of an imagined event, and I wouldn't have to undergo this huge upheaval of everything and everyone I had ever known.

Two days later at dinner, Drew asked me, "Do you think this September is the time we should move to Israel?" I was so surprised that I could only utter the truth without missing a beat.

"Yes," was my simple reply.

This conversation took place in May of 1982. Within three months, we had sold our cars, unloaded a large household of goods, rented out our house, quit two excellent jobs, learned a little conversational Hebrew, and left everything. Closing out our financial, personal and professional lives here felt like preparing for our deaths.

I set my face "like a flint" to put our way of life behind me and steel my resolve to pursue this move with all my heart. Late one night, several weeks before our permanent departure, I was unable to sleep due to the enormity of what I was about to lose. I had a full panic attack which I had never experienced. Fear and anguish gripped me, and my body and mind were wild with an awful expectation of imminent ruin and irreparable loss. I prayed for help and immediately, the Lord led me to Psalm 107, which I had never read before. My eyes were drawn to verse 23:

> *Others went out on the sea in ships; They were merchants on the mighty waters. They saw the works of the LORD, his wonderful deeds in the deep. For he spoke and stirred up a tempest that lifted high the waves. They mounted up to the*

heavens and went down to the depths; In their peril their courage melted away. They reeled and staggered like drunken men; they were at their wits' end. Then they cried out to the LORD in their trouble And he brought them out of their distress. He stilled the storm to a whisper; the waves of the sea were hushed. They were glad when it grew calm, And he guided them to their desired haven (Psalm 107:23-30).

As soon as I had read these words, my spirit grew calm within me. The panic attack immediately vanished. The Lord used His Word to speak to my great fear, and I knew that the unknown was known to Him. I knew He would help us leave safely and establish new lives in Israel. "He would guide us to our desired haven."

We took two suitcases each, a shipment of boxes and two cats. As my mother and I sobbed hysterically in each other's arms at JFK airport, we drew curious stares from many nonchalant passengers waiting to board. Ours, however, was a one-way flight.

CHAPTER 2

SEVEN LEAN YEARS IN THE LAND

About eight months before I knew that we would be moving to Israel, I received a strange warning from the Lord "out of the blue." I was sitting on my bed after a shower, and a clear word came into my mind: *"The time is coming when you will feel that I have abandoned you, but I have not abandoned you."*

While I pondered this word for about a week, I quickly forgot about it, and it was soon "gone with the wind." My faith and trust in the Lord were about to be tested for seven years, and my shallow belief system would be exposed as inadequate.

Our first weeks in Israel were an immersion into a lifestyle of stark simplicity. We received a two-room concrete apartment in a complex for new immigrants called an Absorption Center. These flats contained a two-ring gas burner, a tiny fridge and two steel bed frames with thin foam mattresses. It was unheated, uncarpeted and without a closet or light fixtures. This living arrangement was offered to new immigrants from all nations for six months, in order for them to have a chance to absorb the new culture and language. It was an "interesting" transition after our comfortable home in America. We didn't mind the primitive conditions because we felt like we were on an adventure and we gladly rose to the challenge.

During our first warm September, the dry Mediterranean air was delightful, and the cold stone floors kept us comfortable. The land of Israel is very beautiful, and the climate is pleasant during much of the year. Drew and I began to take Hebrew classes, learned to shop, cook and bank, and we adjusted well to our living arrangements. As I began my life in Israel, my attitude was one of confidence in the Lord because I knew we had moved there out of obedience to a word from Him. I felt adventurous and ready for any hardships that we might encounter; in fact, I was most unprepared and could not have imagined the cost of this unpreparedness.

My first unpleasant surprise took place one night. I got out of bed and walked toward the little kitchen, turning on the light. The floor was alive with cockroaches, scurrying back to their hiding places. I had only seen roaches once in my life while visiting a student in a filthy West Philadelphia hovel. To say that this sight filled me with loathing and terror is an understatement. My fear of the omnipresent Israeli cockroach became a longstanding trauma to my sheltered soul during the five years we lived on the seacoast.

This became an unexpected source of stress to me, and I did not know how to give this fear to the Lord at that time. As my problems began to increase, I found myself pulling back from the Lord; I had learned from childhood to "suffer privately" when things went badly. I did not yet realize that the Lord Jesus wants to hear everything that is in our hearts, even our complaints.

As the weather turned cooler, I began to suffer from a continual chill in the unheated stone apartment. Until the following spring, I could never get warm enough, day or night. The shivering often kept me up all night, no matter how many layers I would wear to bed. I also developed an allergic reaction to an invisible mold spore that grew on the damp walls and suffered asthmatic symptoms and chronic infections for the remainder of our years there. On our first rainy Thanksgiving away from home, I shivered under a blanket and sobbed as I pictured my parents and grandparents gathered for a feast in their warm and welcoming home. Drew had already found a part-time job in electronics, and I was alone in my misery. My homesickness began to gnaw at me, and no amount of brave resolve seemed to mitigate it.

Later, we rented a better concrete apartment, although it too was infested. One night I was sound asleep and for an unknown reason, I suddenly opened my eyes and saw a cockroach racing toward me across the bed. The screams were heard throughout the six-story apartment building. I leapt out of bed shrieking, and at the same time, began to pummel my body with my fists, delivering huge blows of a violent beating to my poor body. I must have thought "it" was on me. The insect had long since disappeared, no doubt frightened away by my screams. My poor husband, who had been awakened out of his usual blissful sleep to find me pounding myself with death blows, was somewhat at a loss as to what to do.

The next morning, I was covered with huge black and green bruises, the pain of which I had not felt the night before due to the remarkable effects of adrenaline. For the next three months, I slept with the lights on and one eye open at all times!

Conception and Deliverance

During our first few months in Israel, I developed an urge to have a baby. At twenty-eight, I was responding to biological signals, and Israeli culture was very conducive to raising children. I had told Drew I wanted a child while we were still living at the Absorption Center. He felt that the conditions of that unpleasant environment were not ideal for conceiving a child and had suggested we wait until we were in our first "real" apartment.

Early in 1983 we attempted to conceive, and five weeks later I was certain I was pregnant; but it turned out I was not, and I found myself very let down. Around this same time, I began a 21-day fast on a special whole-grain bread also found in the book of Ezekiel, called Yahveh's Recipe.[2] My reasons for this lengthy fast were not connected to getting pregnant. I was preparing for my first trip back to the U.S. to visit my parents, and I knew I would encounter strong pressure from them to return home permanently. They had been very opposed to our move to Israel, so I was fasting to prepare my spirit to endure opposition and arguments for moving back.

While fasting, I was reading Francis Schaeffer's book *Genesis in Space and Time.*[3] I came to a section on original sin, in which the author was discussing the curse upon Adam and Eve's bodies caused by their sin. The moment I read this, the Lord brought a strong Word of revelation to me about a curse I had placed on my own body due to sinful attitudes about children. He began to re-mind me of many comments and attitudes I had learned from my parents about the inconvenience of children. They had often remarked that adults had more fun when the children were not around. I also remembered that while in graduate school at the University of Pennsylvania, I had done a research paper on "Child-Free by Choice" couples. This extensive research highlighted a number of couples who explained the multiple reasons why they had made the choice never to bear children. The advantages were numerous, including more money, more time, more vacations and more time with one's spouse.

The Lord showed me a "black" spirit over my heart in this area and gave me an immediate opportunity to repent on the spot. I fully repented at that mo-ment, relinquishing all wrongful belief systems and attitudes concerning chil-dren and families with children. At that moment, I literally felt something dark leave my spirit. The Lord's Spirit instantly spoke to me, saying: *"You are now free to conceive."*

I do not exaggerate when I record that exactly forty weeks from that state-ment, I gave birth to our first child, an adorable blond son. We named him Raviv which means "gentle rains" from the book of Deuteronomy.

My first year with him was like a honeymoon. I nursed him and walked him all over town in his stroller, hanging bags of fruits and vegetables on the handles of the stroller as we shopped in the market each day. Sometimes the bags were too heavy, and the stroller would tip backwards, leaving the baby happily upside down for a moment. Then I would place a bag of sweet potatoes on his lap to balance out the weight and all was well.

I was very happy taking care of him and felt optimistic about our life and future, but as Raviv got older and needed to be bathed in a normal tub, I began to despise this apartment. Among other vexing problems, the bathtub would not drain, and we had a neurotic cat that used the tub as her toilet. I could neither clean the tub properly nor bathe Raviv. We could not modify our cat's behavior or get the drain repaired. Finally, we had to give up the cat and the apartment…we decided to keep Raviv!

The Sin of Hoarding

During these years, our budget was extremely tight. It was hard to decide which essential groceries to buy with such limited money. Due to this pressure and without realizing it, I must have become tight and stingy in order for the following event to take place. To most Americans it will sound ridiculous.

One weekend, we had a guest at our apartment, a dear sister in the Lord. During the weekend, she would snack between meals on what was in our cabinet. She was particularly fond of our prunes.

I'm not sure if other people do this, but for as long as I can remember, we have always had a box of raisins and a box of prunes in the back of our cabinet. No one ever gets them out or eats them, but there they sit, year after year, getting drier but never going bad. I have had prunes from the Nixon administration, and nothing has ever happened to them! This guest ate a lot of our prunes, which we had brought with us from the States and which were as old as sin.

Several months later, she came to visit again. I certainly didn't want her eating all our prunes again, so before she came, I took them out and hid them at the top of a clothing wardrobe. The dear girl stayed for three days, and after she left, I went to the closet to retrieve the prunes.

To my astonishment, every last prune was white with "leprosy," a plague of biblical proportions! As I beheld the hideously diseased prunes, I burst out laughing and declared aloud to the Lord, "You are *so* righteous!" I have never before or after this event seen ancient prunes rot before my eyes.

Needless to say, I have never again been tempted to hide or hoard food. Over the years with a large family and many guests, I have often missed out on something I wanted to eat because the others got to it first. Sometimes my children would write their names on an item so that no one else in the family would take it. But as for me, I would rather lose my earthly treat than lose the pleasure and favor of God upon my life and my possessions. It was not a costly lesson, but it was most effective in changing the heart (Ex. 16:20).

Financial Miracle

Using money from the sale of our house in the States, we purchased a nicer apartment near the Mediterranean Sea. In Israel, homebuyers were required to pay cash for the whole amount, as mortgages were not possible. The morning arrived for the acquisition of the new apartment. I was scheduled to meet the seller at the bank at 8:30 a.m. and bring a large check in US dollars to the foreign currency clerk. This check would then be converted to Israeli shekels for the purchase.

It was one of those dreadful mornings filled with stress and obstacles. First, I overslept, and I struggled to clear my head, which was unusually fogged over. I staggered to the tiny bathroom, but before I could enter, I saw the world's largest cockroach on the white door—the giant species which can fly! I was paralyzed with fear, and I ran from neighbor to neighbor in my nightgown, hoping someone would kill it for me, but to no avail. Someone gave me a can of spray, the kind that requires a huge amount to kill the roach, and not very quickly at that. I was still shaking with fear and drenched in sweat by the time I madly pushed the stroller uphill for a mile to race to the bank. I was very late, and the seller was furious at me.

Then as I began the complicated financial transaction, I saw that the amount of Israeli shekels I received from my dollar check was less than the price I needed to pay the seller. The bank officer explained to me that it had to do with a complex system of unequal exchange rates, but the hard truth was that it was going to cost us our last $300 in the bank to complete the sale. I was shocked and very upset, as I had calculated the amount so carefully. The Lord knew how hard it was for me to accept the loss of our last funds.

Later, when I received the bank statements in the mail, I noticed that the $300 was miraculously still in the account. I went over the figures many times and even talked to the bank to find out why the money had not been taken, but neither I nor any bank officer could explain it. Finally, as I left the bank, I felt the Lord showing me that He had done something mysterious and wonderful to help us in our plight. I thanked Him for His kindness, without ever figuring out how He did it!

Depression and Deliverance

In September of 1985 I became pregnant with our second child. It was a very tough pregnancy. I had tonsillitis ten times during those nine months and was on antibiotics almost continuously. I could not sleep due to the great discomfort. Despite illness and potentially harmful medication, I gave birth to a particularly beautiful and healthy baby girl whom we named Keren, which means "Sunbeam" in Hebrew. As her life has unfolded, Keren's warmth and radiant smile have reflected the attributes of her name. Even now, when we see distinct rays of the sun penetrating a thick bed of clouds to touch the earth, we remember the meaning of her name.

Her birth was very painful, and the anesthesiologist was detained in Tel Aviv's rush-hour traffic and arrived at the hospital after my ordeal was over. After baby Keren's birth, I became severely sleep-deprived and suffered chronic illness for a number of years. This was due to the baby's night schedule, Raviv's morning schedule, and extreme noise factors inside and outside our apartment. I became obsessed with sleep but never got relief.

By the time Keren was about three months old, I started to sink into a prolonged state of lethargy and hopelessness. At first, this depression seemed to be based on my realization of what my life had become. It did not occur to me that I might have a chemical or hormonal imbalance.

The hard reality of day-to-day life in Israel with a toddler and a baby sank in. I was alone in an apartment in what still felt like a foreign country. I missed my mother continually, as we had been extremely close my entire life. I had no relatives or close friends. My Israeli neighbors were decent people, but their extended families were always together, with grandparents and other relatives helping the busy young mothers to raise their children. They had family gatherings on the Jewish holidays and enjoyed a support structure I could never have.

This isolation and loneliness did not bother Drew at all, due to his "loner" personality, as well as his long work days, and regular times of service away from home in Israel's army. He also enjoyed excellent health and slept deeply at night. He had never been close to his parents, nor did he leave behind any close friendships, and therefore was not grieving, afflicted or depressed in any way. He wanted me to pull myself up from the quicksand and just function as evenly and contentedly as he did.

I felt that the life I had chosen was looking grim and hopeless. I felt trapped, alone, bored, neglected and without a future. My only prayers were tears, but I felt that God was angry at me for being discontent. I became like a zombie, going through my days with resignation and futility, like one who has been broken of all hope.

My relationship with God seriously deteriorated at this time and did not fully recover for many years. I was hiding from God because I was ashamed to tell Him that I was sorry I had moved to Israel. Although He was carrying me through this desert of misery, I didn't open my heart to Him. I was in great spiritual danger but couldn't face Him.

It is important for me to add that, despite these mental and physical hardships, I was thankful to have my new baby girl, and I loved her tremendously every single day. She was, and still is, the sweetest and most beautiful creature any mother could wish for. The Lord has designed mothers to have a resilience and enduring love for their little ones, no matter what they are suffering. I would never wish to trade my precious children for any relief, sleep or comfort. Raviv, Keren and Ariela, who would later be born in Jerusalem, were a source of great joy to me and well-worth the temporary hardships I endured.

Long-term sleep deprivation in itself can cause depression, but I did not understand this. While I have heard many stories of classic "post-partem" depression, this seems normally to occur three to six weeks after pregnancy. My depression occurred between the third and seventh month after the birth of my second child. I did not realize this at the time, but I now believe there were hormonal factors concerning the switchover between lactation and the return to my normal menstrual cycle, as I gradually weaned Keren from breastfeeding. Since that time, I have talked to other women who have experienced this later version of post-partem depression. I hope that this condition is now widely understood and discussed in the obstetric community, so that women will not have to suffer this horrible condition without help or understanding.

Over time, I began to realize that I was suffering from depression. This is not obvious to someone experiencing clinical depression for the first time. My husband was not aware of this either. Just admitting this to myself was somehow helpful, although it did not change my condition. One day, I was walking out of my apartment, heading into the center of town for my usual chores. I had the strangest sense of seeing myself from an outside perspective. The thought occurred to me, "You are a woman in a depression. You are going about your chores, anyway." As soon as this thought passed through my mind, it lifted off of me. In one precise moment, walking along that sidewalk, I felt something like a thick blanket of heavy fog lift off of my face and head. It was tangible and physical in its departure. And with that lifting off, a distinct thought entered my mind: "It's over. It's lifted. The depression has been removed." I was lighter, and my mind and heart were restored from that moment.

I found out several days later that a friend of mine, who lived in another town, had been led by the Lord to intercede for me that very day. In her own words, she had prayed for me for seven hours, not even understanding what was wrong with me. I was stunned at the spiritual element of my deliverance from this crippling mental oppression. I honor my old friend, whose name is Candace, and I will always be grateful to her for the sacrifice she made to bring me healing and deliverance.

While I am not in any way opposed to the use of anti-depressants for chronic depression, my experience showed me that the sacrifice of prayer and fasting can break strongholds without the need for medication. The depressed person cannot do this spiritual work alone; prayer "warriors" who love the afflicted ones must "stand in the gap" for them as Candace did for me. In the case of a lactating mother, these drugs are not safe to use anyway and would not have been an appropriate solution for me. If anyone is currently suffering in this manner, please do not ignore it or pretend you are fine. Bring it up to trusted friends, intercessors and medical professionals in order to get the prayer and help you desperately need.

Temptation After the Wilderness

Within a few days of coming out of the wilderness of depression, a dear Christian friend began to pay a great deal of attention to me. He was a missionary to Israel from an American denomination, a married man with a son. When this family had moved to our coastal town almost a year before, I had been very hopeful that his wife would befriend me. I was alone in an apartment most of the day with a toddler and a new baby and really needed a friend. Unfortunately, she was very caught up in social and religious activities with other American women from their denomination and had little interest in spending time with me.

Because I was barely over a lengthy depression, I thought that this man's extra kindness to me was because of the pity he felt for my situation. One day I was walking through town with my ubiquitous stroller and second baby, and I noticed him in his car, watching me. I went over to the car to say "hi." He gazed at me for a long time, and I thought, "He must feel *so* sorry for me!" He then reached his hand through the open window and held my hand for several minutes. I was deeply touched by this affectionate gesture, marveling at his compassion.

As I walked away from the car, I started to feel an unfamiliar tug on my heart. It felt so wonderful for someone to hold my hand and look at me with eyes of caring. This small event triggered an emotional involvement with him that contained elements of secrecy and temptation. This brother's attentiveness was to my arid heart as flashfloods cascading into a desert wadi.

Reminiscent of Yeshua's time of testing after His forty day fast in the desert, my time of temptation also came after a terrible season in the wilderness. It was Satan's strategy to attempt to divert me from my devotion to God, to ruin two marriages, and to bring dishonor and scandal to many in the Lord's Kingdom.

I am eternally grateful to God that we never became physically involved. However, it is possible to experience emotional unfaithfulness, which is a grievous condition in God's eyes. This unhealthy relationship, which lasted about six months, took my emotions from the heights of artificial exhilaration to the depths of suicidal despair. When the impossibility of the relationship sank into my mind, which had turned into the mind of a teenager in love, I was overwrought with grief. Neither of us was righteous in this matter, but I had a significant "fear of the Lord" which protected me from the most destructive course of events.

During this period, it was impossible to worship the Lord in a whole-hearted manner. The distraction and guilt of seeing each other at every fellowship meeting made even my best worship a façade. Nevertheless, the Lord Yeshua never withdrew His love and protection from me, even during this perilous indiscretion. My husband and I were also able to fully recover from this painful breach of trust, for which I am most grateful.

In the end, Drew and I decided to move away from the seacoast town, mainly for reasons of my health, and we relocated to the Jerusalem suburbs. Moving was also an excellent way for me to physically separate from someone who was clearly not part of God's will for my life.

The reason I have included this sinful season of my life, which I would rather have buried in the archives of shame, is because I believe it will help others to avoid this trap. When a married woman feels lonely and neglected, sick, weak or isolated, it is extremely easy for her to succumb to the kind attentions of another man, who gives her all the emotional support she feels she is not receiving from other relationships. Since I was cut off from my parents and had left behind all my close relationships, and because my marriage was not emotionally supportive at that time, I was easily ensnared through depression, isolation and bottomless neediness.

During our two years in Jerusalem I gave birth to my third child, a sweet little girl named Ariela, which means "Lioness of God" in Hebrew. As this exceedingly bright child grew up, her personality developed in accord with her name; Ariela was brave and fiercely confident, intervened on behalf of the weak, and her roar echoed through the jungle of everyday life.

My situation improved a good deal in this new environment, but my health and sleep deprivation did not improve enough to permit me to continue. To my husband's great disappointment and bitter regret, I requested that he take me and the children back to the States, so that I might recover from a physical and emotional burden that I could not sustain. He kindly sacrificed his satisfying life in Israel, and we returned in the summer of 1989.

On the day before we left, I sat alone to pray one final prayer about our time in Israel. I was about to express my gratitude to the Lord that He was relieving me of this long time of suffering. The prayer that my mind had composed was: "Dear Lord, thank You that you are rescuing me from this black hole that has drained every ounce of my strength, money, hope and health."

However, the surprising prayer that popped out of my mouth came, not from my mind, but from the spirit which God had placed inside me:

"Dear Lord, thank You that I have nursed at the breast of Israel for seven years, and that she has nourished and sustained me." This prayer was reminiscent of Isaiah 66, and reflected God's opinion on the matter, which always overrides our selfish and soulish interpretation of events.

Unprepared for Lean Times

As I shared earlier in this chapter, the warning from the Lord was this: *"The time is coming when you will feel that I have abandoned you, but I have not abandoned you."*

As strange as this may sound, I never once remembered this warning during the entire seven years we lived in Israel. During this period, I suffered a profound feeling of abandonment by God. After we had returned to the States, I remembered this word; then I gave glory to the Lord for His kind warning, although it did not seem to benefit me during the lean years of my soul. It reminded me of Peter forgetting the Lord's warning that he would deny Him three times, until after Peter failed the test. It was the same for me.

In those days, I did not record my prayers or experiences with the Lord in a journal, and so this important warning was lost. It is very valuable to record the journey of our relationship with the Lord; He is pleased when His children care enough about the lessons He is teaching them to write them in a journal. I have lost innumerable lessons from my past due to sheer laziness with regard to journaling.

In Genesis 41, we read about Pharaoh's prophetic dreams about seven abundant years and seven "lean years." Joseph interpreted these dreams for Pharaoh and prepared accordingly to provide for an entire nation during seven years of famine.

Although numerous years of financial and emotional abundance were granted me before our move overseas, the "famine" and harshness of these years devoured even the memory of abundance. I was spiritually unprepared for physical suffering, financial hardship, loneliness, the isolation of a mother of young children without support and the cultural and bureaucratic outrages of life in Israel, at least from an American perspective.

While living in comfort, I had assumed that I was a mature believer who was capable of suffering and self-sacrifice during hard times. I was not who I thought I was, and only the sudden immersion into suffering proved the weakness of my faith and strength. I believe that this warning is relevant to all comfortable Christians and Jewish people in this generation—we will be thrust into hardship and suffering which will severely test our strength, integrity and faith. Most of us will not be prepared and will not have time to prepare at that late moment. Just as Joseph could not have begun his preparations once the famine was upon the land, so we cannot afford to wait until the hardship begins for this nation, our churches and our families. At that time, it will be too late to prepare.

The stress, illness and depression wore away my trust in the Lord and my marriage. I became hopeless and was tempted by sins which under "normal" circumstances would not interest me. I did not have the extra "oil in my lamp," described in the parable of the ten virgins in Matthew 25, necessary to keep the light in my spirit burning brightly with hope, perseverance and enduring trust. I am grateful that I did not have to face His Judgment Throne at that point in my life. Truly, my lamp had gone out, and I tremble to think what words I might have heard from Him on that day. Had I truly allowed Him to know me, as the Scripture requires?

Perhaps if I had remembered the Lord's earlier warning, as I encountered hardships during those years, I would have become an overcomer rather than being overcome by my circumstances.

I have told you these things, so that in me you may have peace. In this world you will have trouble. But take heart! I have overcome the world (John 16:33).

On Earth as It Is in Heaven

After returning to the States, it took me a long time to receive complete healing and restoration from the Lord. I felt ashamed that I had failed my "wilderness test." I had utterly failed to demonstrate faith in His goodness and His ability to bring good out of bad circumstances. I also felt like a failure for not making a successful life in the land of Israel, where the Lord had called us. I wondered what future ministry I had thrown away due to my endless illness, stress, sleep deprivation and depression.

I did not realize that the difficult and miraculous experiences I encountered during those years would yield a great harvest of fruitfulness later in my life. Living seeds of truth and understanding were planted by the Lord deep in my heart throughout this season, and they did not die; they took root, grew with the watering of His Word and the stimulation of His Spirit, and accomplished the good purposes for which He planted them.

As we left the land of Israel, my human reasoning told me that nothing good had come out of this "black hole" in my life. I was prepared to thank the Lord for rescuing me out of a destructive and draining environment, one which had sucked up and absorbed my strength and health. But my spirit, which was connected to God's purposes in my life, prayed:

"Dear Lord, thank You that I have nursed at the breast of Israel for seven years and that she has nourished and sustained me."

The true nourishment that I received in Israel during those seven years was not apparent to me while my suffering dulled my vision and perspective. The Lord was planting imperishable seed in me, but the fulfillment and realization of this fruit would not become evident for many years. The Lord Yeshua taught us to pray, "Let Your Kingdom come; Let Your will be done on earth, as it is in heaven." What God has decreed in heaven is often not accomplished immediately in the earthly realm but is realized over time with repentance, intercession and the full agreement of His people.

We see this model in 1 Kings 18 and in the Book of Esther. In the days of Ahab and Jezebel, the worship of Baal had brought a curse over the Land; there had been no rain for three years, and the wicked king blamed the prophet Elijah for this trouble. After the showdown on Mount Carmel, the people knew that the Lord was God, for He alone sent fire from heaven to consume the sacrifice. After the prophets of Baal were slain, the curse of the drought was broken; however, Elijah still needed to intercede for rain and before even a tiny cloud was sighted, he declared to Ahab, "There is the sound of a heavy rain." He saw in the Spirit what was not yet a physical reality on earth.

Likewise, in the Book of Esther, we see Haman's evil decree of slaughter published throughout the Persian empire; Mordechai responded with sackcloth and wailing in the streets and outside the king's gate. After he persuaded Esther to intercede before the King, all of the Jews fasted and prayed for her protection and for this slaughter to be stopped. Esther rose up to judge Haman and the arrogant ruler was hanged. However, while the curse had been broken, the reality of Persian law was that the day of slaughter could not be revoked; a real battle on the ground still needed to take place in the future.

The appointed day of Haman's proposed slaughter finally arrived, but the Jewish people, who had now been given permission to assemble and arm themselves, gained the victory over their enemies. The earthly realization did not take place at the same moment that Heaven intervened in favor of the Jewish people and decreed their victory.

As with these two scriptural examples, in the fullness of time, the Lord produced in my life the harvest of His blessings and purposes, which He had decreed for those seemingly fruitless years; the earthly fruit ripened long after the heavenly command had come to me, a single word: *"Israel."*

He has made everything beautiful in its time. He has also set eternity in the hearts of men; yet they cannot fathom what God has done from beginning to end (Ecclesiastes 3:11).

The Lord's Goodness in Dark Times

The Lord was incredibly kind and gentle towards me after our return. He never once accused me or said that He was disappointed with me, although I was very disappointed with myself. He readily forgave me for my numerous bad attitudes and lack of trust in Him. While I expected punishment, I received nothing but kindness upon blessing upon mercy. This is the kind of Savior we have the privilege to serve. Truly, there is *no* condemnation to those who are in Messiah Yeshua! (Rom 8:1)

I am still amazed at the way He treated me after my terrible failure. Finally, I had to simply accept myself as I accepted His restoration, knowing that He did not want me to continue to feel like a failure or to endlessly repent for my faithlessness. When the Lord restores His child, He does it wonderfully and completely.

Several very good things came out of those lean years as well. I found fellowship with lovely Jewish and Gentile believers who lived in Israel. Drew and I were able to experience several of the Messianic congregations in the Tel Aviv and Jerusalem areas, most of which are still thriving to this day; we also met believers from all over the world and built friendships with them. We had many guests stay with us over the years and were able to extend help to those in need. I had the privilege of ministering to a Jewish immigrant from Iran and her son, and she received the Lord as we prayed together.

The Lord gave me a number of new worship songs, some of which were in Hebrew for the Israeli children. I was also able to record a second cassette project of my songs in a Jerusalem studio owned by believers. (Recently, I was able to put the best of these two song collections onto CD.) I also learned many awesome songs written by Israeli believers, which have helped me to memorize Scripture in Hebrew.

The experiences of life in Israel, as well as the immersion into the Hebrew language, have proven very valuable to me as a Bible teacher and psalmist. In addition, the Lord gave us three amazing children who are citizens of Israel as well as U.S. citizens. Through hardship, I learned to adapt to a culture and lifestyle which is far removed from the comforts and luxury of life in the U.S. Despite my complaints, I learned much patience and endurance, and for these I am now grateful.

Finally, I was able to observe and experience firsthand the difficulties of being an Israeli citizen; we have been hated and hunted by the Lord's enemies and misjudged by nations who knew little of terrorism in earlier decades. Even in these days when many other nations have experienced the cruelty of terrorism on their own soil, there remains a double-standard when it comes to

Israel's response to terrorism on her own soil. What other nations would not and do not tolerate, Israel is expected to quietly accept. I experienced the hypocrisy of the nations as an Israeli.

Despite these obstacles, "all Israel will be saved" when "the Spirit is poured upon us from on high, and the desert becomes a fertile field." We will reap a harvest of deliverance and righteousness for the glory of His name and His covenant-keeping reputation (Rom. 11:26, Isa. 32:15, Ezek. 36:22-23).[4]

The Church Must Prepare for Lean Times

Lean years can be described as a long period of grief or frustration; these are years which we cannot wait to be over. We desperately look forward to an end of these times of "famine," assuming we have enough hope to believe that they will come to a happy end at some point. A time is coming when the only true hope for the suffering to end, will be the return of the Lord Yeshua to rescue those who love His appearing and have made themselves ready for Him (2 Tim. 4:8; Rev. 19:7).

Fat, abundant years can feel like "normal" times. Often we enjoy each day, or at least live it to the fullest, with no thought of storing up physical or spiritual resources for a future time of hardship. When we are full, it is nearly impossible to imagine true hunger; when we are hungry, it is nearly impossible to remember abundance. But those few who survived the concentration camps will never forget. Some carry food with them at all times, due to the endless memory of cruel starvation.

In keeping with the startling warning I received more than twenty years ago, I believe that a time is coming when His people will feel that He has abandoned them, but He has not abandoned them. The six hours that Jesus hung on the tree must have been the longest hours in history. Surely He felt abandoned and forsaken by His Father (Matt. 27:46). In truth, He was not abandoned, but He felt that way. God delivered His soul from death at the proper time.

It will be the same with the time of testing for God's people. Store up oil in your lamps, which is the Presence and daily infilling of the Holy Spirit, and set daily time aside for intimate and heartfelt worship to the Father and Yeshua, our great High Priest who cares for the welfare of our souls. Tell Him every sorrow and complaint of your heart, as well as your appreciation and love for Him. Never hide your face from Him. For the Lord Jesus to truly and intimately know us, we must bare our thoughts to Him in complete transparency.

A righteous man may have many troubles, but the Lord delivers him from them all (Psalm 34:19).

CHAPTER 3

"MY CHILDREN DON'T WANT ME!"

We returned to the States in the middle of 1989. The children were ages five, three and one at the time. For about two years, I was continually recovering from the intense seven-year period of life in Israel.

During these first few years back, the Lord began a lengthy process of blessing, enlarging, healing and restoring me. Most of my physical problems were healed, and gradually the endless weeping subsided. Upon returning, we immediately found a large and caring church, which our family attended for about six years. Through involvement in this church, I was finally able to "rest" in the goodness of God, enjoy worship, and find healthy and supportive friendships.

Finally, I began to regain my mental and emotional balance. Although I never sought leadership responsibilities, I was gradually asked to serve in musical and teaching ministries. This allowed me to give back to this wonderful church a small amount of what I had received from them during the painful years of recovery.

In addition to my spiritual recovery, the Lord also gradually restored our family's financial health, which had been severely depleted by the cost of living in Israel. He opened many doors of blessing to our growing children and helped us with many medical, educational and spiritual decisions concerning their lives and development. I am exceedingly grateful for His continual help and guidance with our son and two daughters as we adjusted to a new life yet again.

In the fall of 1993, I reluctantly accepted my first long-term teaching assignment at my church. I was nervous about this responsibility, seeing it as an academic discipline which would require rigorous Bible study and articulate presentations. I never imagined the anointing the Lord would begin to pour out on my teachings over the many years to come, as I gradually learned to rely on His Spirit to fill and empower my words. Nor could I have guessed or even hoped for the life-altering visitation of His manifest glory I was about to receive.

The Visitation

It was between the Feasts of Rosh Hashannah and Yom Kippur of 1993, and I had taught my first class. It was a Sunday night in September, and I was asleep.

I got up in the middle of the night to go to the bathroom, went back to bed and just lay there, peaceful and very much awake. Normally, I would lie awake and worry about whether or not I would fall back to sleep. Due to a persistent sleep disorder, it was very common for me to awaken between two and four a.m. and never get back to sleep. In those days, it did not occur to me to pray during these wakeful night hours. On this occasion I was not worried about how I would face the next day.

What happened next was so unfamiliar to my Christian or Jewish knowledge base that I had no vocabulary at the time to describe it. As I lay there with eyes open, thinking about nothing in particular, I was suddenly thrust into another realm; it was as if there were another "version" of myself, kneeling in fervent, intense prayer in some unknown location. I now believe that what the Apostle John describes as being "in the Spirit" is what seemed to be another version of myself (Rev. 1:10). I was kneeling between two tall men to whom I could not turn my head to study but only saw out of my peripheral vision. They were standing resolutely on either side of me. I somehow knew that they had been interceding for me for hours and that, because of their faithful and lengthy prayers for me, whatever I asked for in prayer at that moment would be instantly granted. My physical body was still lying on the bed, but I was more connected to the part of me that was kneeling between the two men.

I was praying with a desperation and intensity that I had never come close to praying in "real life," where my prayers were at best, emotional, and at worst, lifeless. I knew that the moment I asked, it would be granted to me, but I had no decision-making capability as to what I should ask for. The prayer just burst out of my mouth, without premeditation:

"Oh, Lord, come to me!"

The second those words left my lips, He immediately answered them. His Presence came over me like a powerful cloud, surrounding and filling my mind and body with a thick and weighty euphoria that was completely unknown to me in the nineteen years I thought I had known Him. The effect on my body was wonderfully ecstatic and utterly unfamiliar, and continued to increase in strength for what seemed like many minutes. For a while, I welcomed this Presence and prayed for more, but as it grew, it began to frighten me with its relentless intensity. At some point, I felt my flesh "dissolve" under the power, and my legs seemed to turn to jelly.

During this period of time, I was aware of God communicating knowledge

to me directly. I will attempt to convey in words the knowledge given to me
while under this Presence:

"Do you think if you were standing right now, your legs would hold you up?"

"No." (My answers were in thoughts, not words.) I saw the people at my
church, standing in worship and singing to God.

*"The people at your church, when they ask Me to come to them and reveal My
glory to them, do you think they want Me to do to them what I am doing to you
right now?"*

I felt sad, realizing that this experience was very uncomfortable and that
most Christians would not want what they think they are asking for.

"No," I answered.

"If I did this to them, would they still be standing up and singing songs?"

"No." I saw the undignified scene of hundreds falling to the floor on their
faces and realized it would be an embarrassment which would not be desired.
What if visitors were driven away by this spectacle?

*"When people ask Me to come, they do not know what they are asking for.
They do not want the 'real Me.' This is what it feels like when the 'real Me' over-
shadows you. It is too intense and frightening, and My people do not actually want
Me."*

Again, I felt His sadness that He was rejected by His own church due to the
discomfort of being in His Manifest Presence. I knew that the biblical word in
Hebrew for "glory" is Kavod, which literally means heaviness or weight. It is indeed a weight capable of crushing our frail human frames if He so desired.

During this visitation, the Lord reminded me of my criticisms and judgments
of the physical manifestations of the "Toronto Revival," which was a controversial
topic at that time. Friends had sent me scholarly articles which disparaged these
manifestations as unbiblical and even demonic. I myself had even made somewhat negative remarks about people being "slain in the Spirit." Never, in my years
of knowing Yeshua, had I ever felt a power even close to the point of being unable
to stand. It had seemed like hype and emotional manipulation.

I knew that men of God fell down in His Presence in the Bible, but my life
in Him was dry, full of head knowledge and devoid of power; therefore, I could
only conclude that the "Toronto experience" was a movement bent on experien-
tial extremism. Needless to say, through this experience, the Lord was ensuring
that I would never again criticize that which I did not understand. Discernment
would always continue to be an important part of my walk and teaching, but I
would be much more humble and cautious in the future about criticizing another ministry without extensive understanding of the situation.

I then asked God two questions about what was happening. I was aware of
lying in bed, overcome with the uselessness of my body, but I was also still
kneeling between the two men, who were standing as steady as ever.

"Why aren't the two men falling down? How can they keep standing with this power over us?" I did not receive an answer to this question. I now believe that "they" (angels or living saints in heaven) are accustomed to standing in the glory and therefore, can bear to stand.

As my husband remained asleep next to me, my second question was, "If You are truly in this room at this level of power, how can Drew sleep peacefully through this?" His answer came:

"Two people can be lying in a bed, and My shadow can pass over one and not the other. Two people can be standing in a field, and my cloud can cover one and not the other. I can make a distinction between people."

When my fear had increased to the point that I felt that I would physically die under this unbearable power, I said, "Lord, I can't take it anymore." The moment this fearful prayer was uttered by my heart, His shadow began to pass over me, as a cloud is blown away on a windy day. He gradually left, and I came back to a sense of normalcy, lying in my bed. My legs were still disabled with a useless and tingly feeling for quite a while after His Presence departed. The kneeling version of me and the two faithful men did not seem to exist anymore.

When the morning came, I questioned what had happened to me. Did God really come into my room in such tremendous power that I thought I would die? If that was God, why was I terrified, and why did I send Him away? Should a person be afraid if it is our wonderful Lord? Could it have been Satan? I told Drew everything about the visitation, having no idea if he would believe me. He said that all of it sounded biblical. That was comforting to me, and I appreciated his support at a moment of questioning.

I wondered if I was supposed to share this experience with my regular class at church. I sensed in my spirit that this testimony was only to be shared when He prompted me to tell it and that it was not to be shared freely. As I got up to speak in the morning class, I was certain that I was not to share it at that time. But later that night, I had to teach a different group from the same church. I felt the Lord release me to share it in that class and I obeyed. It was well-received by the leadership and was very helpful to at least one person in the room. While I was driving home that night, I knew with absolute certainty that this experience was real and was from God Himself. I have never questioned it since.

It would be eleven more years before I would experience His glory again. During these long years, I would regret having asked Him to leave; I promised Him repeatedly that if He ever visited me again, I would never send Him away, even if it killed me. As Queen Esther said bravely, "If I perish, I perish." To this day, I have kept my sacred promise to Him.

PART II

BEING KNOWN BY GOD

CHAPTER 4

DECEPTIVE COUNTERFEITS

The eleven years, during which I regretted sending His glory away and prayed that He would return, were certainly not unproductive years. They were fully occupied with many tasks, which were always being balanced and prioritized. We were raising the three children, and I was working to help our family afford their Christian school tuition; I was also giving private piano and guitar lessons and home-schooling two of the children during different years. In ministry, I taught the Bible, wrote articles, led worship and composed songs; I also conducted special teachings and events connected to the Feasts of the Lord and Passover Seders, which Drew and I led together every spring.

My walk with the Lord was fairly healthy during this period, although I had not yet learned to openly tell Him everything I was thinking and feeling, nor had I learned how to wait on Him in intimate fellowship and expectancy. I did not yet understand the bridal, love relationship with Yeshua that He desired and was eager to reveal, not only to me, but to all of His beloved children who long for Him above all things. This revelation of intimate friendship, which I began to receive in 2004 and which has accelerated significantly since that time, is the very purpose for which this book was written. There is not one of His children who cannot walk in this astonishingly real and passionate relationship with the Lord Jesus our Messiah. (This will be explored much more in the next few chapters.)

There was one very significant experience which occurred in October of 2003 which is too important to omit from my life's testimony. This took place during the fall biblical feasts, but I did not record the exact date it occurred. I was sleeping in bed; at 5:00 a.m., I suddenly felt my heart stop with a violent jolt, but there was absolutely no pain. If there had been pain, I would have thought it was a real heart attack and gone to the emergency room. But I clearly felt my heart stop with great force. Then I suddenly saw the date, "20XX" written in front of my closed eyes. (I cannot publish the actual year I was shown.) I was still healthy and now wide awake, and I knew that my heart must have started beating normally again. I assumed He was telling me that I would physically die in that year. I treasured this in my heart, only telling a few trusted people. This information would prove to be helpful several years later, when I would receive additional revelation about my destiny.

Mitzi's Salvation

There is one other significant experience I believe the Lord wishes me to include, which occurred at the end of this transitional phase of my life. I am including this brief testimony concerning my mother Mitzi's passing, which occurred in the first weeks of 2005.

Having received the Lord in 1973, I had shared my faith with both my parents for many years, but nothing I said ever penetrated their worldview. Part of the obstacle was being Jewish, but part of it was the liberal and humanistic thought system which was far too entrenched in them to be dislodged. If any words could have persuaded, surely I could have brought those words to bear with a knowledge level that they both respected very much.

Even so, the mind can hear excellent truth without the heart turning in a radically different direction. The image in the liberal Jewish mind of "Jesus hanging on the cross" is viewed as foreign and Catholic, and is dismissed utterly. To see Yeshua's sacrificial death in the light of our own Hebrew Scriptures, and to acknowledge His wholly Jewish identity would require a humility and openness which my parents could not muster. An additional problem was that they were not familiar with their own Hebrew Scriptures, and my lengthy explanations were not desired.

My father Irv passed away in 1996 and sadly, I have no evidence that he received the Lord Yeshua before he died. Mitzi was madly in love with him, and she suffered the deep grief of his loss privately, while moving bravely forward in her responsibilities.

She was a strong and adorable woman who never looked even close to her actual age. Both Mitzi and Irv shared an outrageous perspective, which was that neither of them would ever die. I realize that this defies common sense, but somehow they managed to hold onto this optimistic view. Of course, they made necessary legal preparations, but in their hearts, it was theoretical. This made it very hard for me to ask questions like, "What do you think will happen when you die?"

Mitzi was stricken suddenly and without warning with a ruptured blood vessel in the brain; she developed the worst headache she had ever felt and called me at work. By the time I arrived at her house, she was lying on the couch with slurred speech and unable to move her left arm. She was taken to the hospital, and within one hour, her CAT scan showed the brain rapidly filling with blood, already half gone; she was unconscious by the time I got to her side.

It was unreal to hear the doctor say that she would not recover from this, since the whole event was so sudden; she went from having a headache to dying within two hours. Like Israeli Prime Minister Ariel Sharon, Mitzi was on blood thinners, and this makes a cerebral hemorrhage deadly and quick.

I sent the others out of the room, and I began to cry and to tell her that it was still not too late to receive Yeshua. I had learned that unconscious people can still hear, and it was worth trying. I pleaded, "Even now, Mom, we don't have to be separated for all time. Even now, He will receive you if you will receive Him." I said a bit more, but I cannot remember my words. I know it was not a complete presentation of the atonement of Yeshua; I was focusing on the possibility that we could still be together forever, and I was in too much shock to think straight. Thankfully, I had told her a lot over the years, and she may have remembered some of it.

When I finished making my final offer, I said, "Mom, if you have understood every word I said, squeeze my hand really hard." I held my breath and waited; after about two seconds, she gave me a good, hard squeeze! I thanked her and told her that I felt that.

I looked at Mitzi's face and saw tears forming at the corners of her eyes. I had not seen these tears moments before, and I believe her heart was responding to what she had heard and understood. I tried to recite Psalm 23, which was the only Psalm she knew from childhood. I told her we would be together in heaven. Mitzi died the next morning.

About a week or two later, I was grieving, and I said to the Lord, "Is this the only assurance I have, Lord, after thirty years? Is this all I have to hold onto, a squeeze of the hand?"

The Lord said to me, *"Which hand did she squeeze you with?"*

To my astonishment, I realized I had been standing at her left side. Before we had even left her house, she was unable to move her left arm! I knew it was even more of a miracle that she was able to use her left hand than if she had responded with her other side. I was then satisfied that Mitzi received the Lord before she died, and I thank Him for showing her mercy at this critical last moment. Praise His name!

God's Glory Returns

During the summer of 2004, I was attending an anointed conference where the worship was intense, and the message of God's love for Israel was strongly emphasized. For about an hour, I poured out my deepest worship to Him with "all my heart and all my strength." This commandment, found in Deuteronomy 6:4, was considered to be the "greatest commandment" by our Lord Jesus.

During the period of worship, one of my dear friends felt led by the Holy Spirit to anoint my feet; while I received this kindness with joy, it did not distract me from my devotion to God. This anointing may have contributed to what happened next, though I cannot be certain.

After worship, I sat down with all the others for the message to be preached. While the general atmosphere in the meeting seemed to return to "normal" as the announcements and message were presented, I began to experience the tangible glory of God for which I had been hoping and waiting during the last eleven years. I stayed in that overwhelming Presence all through the preaching, which I barely heard. I remained in my chair, still immobilized, for 45 minutes after the meeting ended. The dry season was over, and the "latter rains" of His Spirit, spoken by the prophet Joel, had begun in my life.

From that point on, I was graced to receive more visitations of this nature with increasing frequency. During the remainder of 2004, these extraordinary experiences were still widely separated by many months. But as 2005 progressed, I noticed them coming more frequently and could be compared to "birth pains." They seemed to happen most often during a small prayer and worship time we held every Shabbat (Saturday morning). Each week, four or five intercessors would meet at our church or at my home for fervent worship and prayer for regional, national and international issues; in particular, we regularly interceded for the salvation of Israel and the Jewish people, as taught in Romans 11.

I believe that the Lord is very pleased with these offerings on the seventh day, which God declared at creation to be the Sabbath (in Hebrew, *Shabbat*). In speaking of the biblical Sabbath, I neither feel nor imply any criticism of Sunday worship, which is wholly pleasing to our Lord when conducted with reverent awe, holiness and zeal. His children are free to worship Him every day of the week. I myself participate joyfully in Sunday worship every week at my church or as a guest if I am teaching somewhere else; I also observe the seventh day as *kadosh* (set apart) for the Lord, as His Word instructs.

Just before the fall of 2005, a large increase took place in the frequency and strength of these experiences. I watched a series of teachings on DVD by a dear brother from India, named Sadhu Sundar Selvaraj, called "The Art of Waiting on God."[5] These fascinating teachings explained how it is critically important for all believers to wait in the Lord's presence. We are to put off all distracting thoughts and activities and wait quietly for Him to renew our strength and reveal Himself to us, as taught in Isaiah 40. I had been waiting on Him before I heard these teachings, but not at the level of concentration or length of time I began to practice after hearing them.

The first day that I tried waiting in the long silence, I placed my *tallit* (the

Jewish prayer shawl) on my head with the sides hanging straight down on either side of my head. I closed my eyes and sat perfectly vertical and still in my rocking chair. I waited, barely breathing. During the next ten minutes, the strangest thing happened. First, I felt the prayer shawl begin to slip forward on my head. Physically, this did not seem logical, as the weight of the shawl was not in the front, and I was vertical and still. I thought perhaps it was just slippery and was sliding a bit. Then it moved more. As the minutes went by, it seemed to be inexorably moving down my forehead, and the sides seemed to be closing in on my face. I felt excited but a little afraid of what was happening. I resisted the urge to move my arms upward to feel or adjust the prayer shawl. Finally, to my astonishment, the two sides of the tallit moved improbably and dramatically across my face like the curtains being closed in a movie theatre.

The moment my face was fully covered, the glory fell upon me, and I remained in the awe and incapacitation of that power for about an hour. I remembered the verse that says that the Seraphim have six wings, and with two, they cover their faces (Isa. 6:2). So I knew it was biblical to cover one's face in the presence of Almighty God.

The next day, I couldn't wait to get to my rocking chair. I carefully placed the prayer shawl on my head, as vertical as humanly possible and waited breathlessly. Nothing happened. After ten minutes, not a molecule had budged, and I was disappointed. Then I heard the Holy Spirit say, *"Cover your own face."* I realized He was not going to move it supernaturally every day; He only did that on the first day so that I would understand His desire for my face to be covered. After that, it was my responsibility. So, of course, I covered my face in the same way and again, His most marvelous and incomprehensible glory came upon me and lasted close to an hour.

This same pattern continued for about a month, coming every day with breathtaking power. I began to think it would continue like this every day, for the rest of my life. I was fully addicted to the indescribable pleasure, fear and incapacitating power of His Manifest Presence. No pleasure or distraction on this earth could be remotely compared to the reality of His glory. Who could want anything less?

Then the Feast of Trumpets arrived on October 4, 2005 (also called *Rosh Hashannah*). A group of intercessors and I were to fly out to Birmingham, Alabama, that day, to attend an intercessory and repentance conference.[6] The purpose of this gathering was to weep and deeply repent of the innocent blood of African Americans shed on our soil during the 100 years following the Emancipation Proclamation. During this shameful period after the Civil War, thousands of African Americans were cruelly lynched without a trial, and a variety of crushing injustices were imposed on a supposedly "freed" people, protected under our Constitution.

The repentance that takes place in these painful gatherings is vitally important for the delaying of God's judgments against our nation. He cannot ignore the blood of the innocent that has been shed in a nation's history, even if He waits many years. There will either be repentance or judgment; this is a fully biblical truth. Even so, the coming judgments, while having been delayed by God's mercy, are not cancelled against this nation.

That morning before our flight, I waited in my rocking chair, expecting the visit of His glory which had come every day for a month. It never came; I waited for an hour and never felt anything. I burst into tears and wondered what had happened. I knew I had not done anything wrong or different that would explain why He didn't show up in a tangible way. While I never received an explanation from the Lord for this lack of glory, nor did He owe me an explanation, I now believe that He has sovereign purposes for every phase of our growth and instruction. There are times in our lives for training, study of His Word, receiving His kindness, patient endurance, discipline, correction and various spiritual rewards that keep us encouraged and excited about Him. It would seem that the amazing and glorious month I enjoyed with the Lord was a special reward to boost my faith, show me His power, and ruin me for any worldly pleasure forever. He accomplished His purpose, for I am indeed ruined.

The Warning Comes

It was two days before we were to leave for Birmingham and also two days before the Feast of Trumpets. It was a Sunday night and I was asleep. At 1:00 a.m. I was abruptly awakened out of a deep sleep by the voice of the Lord:

"Satan has demanded permission to tempt you sexually, and I have granted it."

I was shocked by this warning, although it reminded me of the Lord's warning to Peter (Luke 22:31-32). In thirty years as a believer, I had never received a warning of this sort; as I lay there in bed, pondering this strange word, I tried to figure out the way this temptation would take place. I thought I could outwit Satan by working it all out ahead of time and then just avoiding the tempting situation. This was a foolish first response, but that was how my mind worked.

Since I was traveling to Birmingham with three other women and one man, I assumed the temptation would be connected to the man. He was a dear friend, and I just assumed that somehow, an unhealthy situation would arise in this relationship. Thus, I reasoned that if I just stayed away from him, I would be fine. After several minutes of this human reasoning, the Lord showed me that it would not help me to prepare for this test by figuring it out; rather, I needed to pray for my own protection and deliverance from evil as taught by the Lord

Yeshua in Matthew 6:13, as well as in Luke 22:40 and 46. Peter was warned of Satan's demand, but the Lord prayed for him and twice told Peter to pray that he would not fall into temptation.

Finally, I got out of bed and knelt to pray. I put on all my spiritual armor as taught in Ephesians and prayed against every scheme of the evil one. I prayed that I would pass this test and would do nothing to make the Lord ashamed of me, or make me ashamed of myself. I could not think of anything more I could do to prepare for whatever was coming, and so I returned to bed.

Two days later, we flew to Birmingham. My roommate and I checked into our hotel room, and all the others checked into their respective rooms. We arrived on a Tuesday afternoon, and the conference did not begin until Wednesday morning. We went to bed that night, and I slept until 4:00 A.M. Wednesday morning.

Before I share the testimony of this first temptation, I need to explain one particular manifestation of God's Presence, as it has affected my body at times. If this is not clear to the reader from the beginning, my description of this temptation will seem like an obvious Satanic attack, and the reader will wonder why in the world a mature believer could not discern what was happening.

From the time I began to receive visitations of God's glory, I have noticed several ways my body responds to His power, including being perfectly still at times. The word for "spirit" in Hebrew is *ruach*, which means wind or spirit. In Greek, it is *pneuma*, which has the same meaning. From this Greek root we derive the words "pneumatic" and "pneumonia," both relating to air pressure or breath.

We are all accustomed to breathing and know what it means to take an exceptionally deep breath. For example, while swimming, we will deliberately take a large breath and fill our lungs to capacity if we need to go a distance underwater. At other times, we will involuntarily heave a large sigh at a time of overwhelming emotion. Sometimes, these deep sighs are accompanied by shuddering or trembling. As we sigh, we take an enormous breath, and feel our chest cavity expand.

In a similar way, while waiting on the Lord or spending time worshiping Him with strong focus, I will sometimes feel Him expand my inward space. I am not referring to physical breath because most often, my body is very still, and my breathing is shallow and minimal. But as His Spirit moves in me in a powerful way, I feel the area from my stomach into my chest cavity begin to expand, as if being inflated by a source of air pressure. This is a pleasant and not a frightening sensation (Eph. 5:18).

This expansion can continue until I am filled and feel that I could explode, at which point there is a release of pressure. This release can include trembling or muscular contractions of a non-violent nature. Sometimes, it is like sobbing, but without sorrow or tears. It is as if my flesh cannot contain the energy and activity of His Spirit, and it reaches a breaking point. After the release, the Lord might fill me again, although each interaction with Him is unique and wholly unpredictable. He is directing this activity, and it is not worked up by my human effort.

In some instances, my stomach muscles will get very tight, as if I were doing abdominal crunches. My shoulders and back muscles can tighten as well. This may sound like a contradiction, but in one sense these movements are involuntary, and yet I am voluntarily yielding to the Lord's Spirit to permit them to occur.

While the thought of involuntary movements could have a frightening or pathological connotation, I am testifying that this can happen in the Spirit to a normal, healthy person who has no such abnormal movements during the regular activities of life. I would also like to add that when the Holy Spirit is doing this work, I could decide at any point not to yield to this activity, and it would stop. He requires our voluntary participation in everything He wishes to do in our lives. He never manipulates us in any way. (For the distinguishing features of some of the diverse manifestations of the Lord's Presence, see Chapter 8 in the section entitled, "The Secret Place of the Most High.")

At first, these manifestations concerned me. I did not want to get caught up in any counterfeit experiences which were carnal or even demonic. Over a long period of time, after much testing and observation of the fruits of this activity, I became convinced that this was of His Spirit. Although I am still growing, the good and imperishable fruit of the Spirit is evident in my life, and we are cautioned by our Lord, "By their fruit you will recognize them" (Matt. 7:16).

We read many biblical accounts of the physical effects of God's glory on the patriarchs and prophets (Dan. 7:17-18, 27, 10:7-10, 15-19; Rev. 1:17, Ezek. 1:28-2:2, 8:3; Is. 66:2; Ex. 19:16). I have also known other credible believers who experience similar manifestations; it is important to test all experiences with His written Word, and to welcome all activity which is of His Spirit. The following trial indicates the importance of testing all things, and the power of His Word to dispel a counterfeit manifestation, when spoken aloud.

But the fruit of the Spirit is love, joy, peace, patience, kindness, goodness, faithfulness, gentleness and self-control. Against such things there is no law (Galatians 5:22-23).

The Sexual Test

When I awoke at 4:00 that Wednesday morning, I quietly got out of bed to wait on the Lord without disturbing my friend. I sat in a chair, wearing my tallit, and spent time with Him until 5:20 A.M. During this time, I experienced the sensations described above, which often accompany my times in His Presence. I then felt very tired and went back to bed, hoping to sleep for another hour before we had to get ready for the morning meeting.

The moment I lay down on the bed, I began to experience spasms which were somewhat like the involuntary movements I have just described, but they seemed to originate more in the pelvic region. A pleasurable sensation began to come over me, which was not entirely different from the pleasure I feel when I am in the Lord's presence.

It is important to understand the difference between the enjoyment that flows from God's heart to His children, and the counterfeit, sensual pleasure which comes from the adversary. The Lord is not in a competition with the enemy to see who can give us a more satisfying experience. The delight we sometimes feel in God's Presence could be viewed as a benefit of His glory, love and power. The Lord's primary purpose is not to give us good feelings, but to intimately commune with us. The love that flows between beloved friends or the intimacy which finds expression between a husband and wife, produces a flood of joyful chemistry (Song of Songs 1:2, 4:10). The Scriptures tell us that there is joy in His presence and pleasures at His right hand forevermore (Psalm 16:11).

Satan, on the other hand, will use any tool, including pleasure, to accuse, shame and discredit God's people. At times he is granted by the Lord temporary and limited permission to send a deceptive enticement or fiery trial upon those whom he wishes to seduce, attack and lead away into destruction (Job 1:11-12, 2:6, 1 Pet. 5:8).

As we learn from Job's trial, Peter's temptation, and that of Jesus Himself, the Lord can choose to grant Satan limited opportunity to harm or test His people (Luke 22:31, Matt. 4:1-11). It is not the purpose of this writing to explain why this happens, but the best explanation is the book of Job itself. Job had no control over the affliction that came upon him, but how he responded to it was the test.

At that early moment, as I experienced this unfamiliar sensation, the differ-ence between the good and the counterfeit was too subtle for me to discern. As this manifestation began, I naively believed it was a continuation of what was happening to me while I had waited on the Lord, just moments before. Because I thought it was of God, I did not attempt to rebuke it right away.

It is uncomfortable for me to describe this experience, and I have limited my descriptions so that God will be glorified in all that I say. My purpose for openly and honestly sharing this is to bring a clear warning to others, so that the holy and the profane will be clearly distinguished, and none of His children, male or female, will be deceived. There is great seduction and deception coming upon His people in the area of sensuality, and He desires intensely that His people not be ignorant of Satan's devices. Thus, I am voluntarily transparent for the sake of His flock.

The Spirit clearly says that in later times some will abandon the faith and follow deceiving spirits and things taught by demons (1 Tim. 4:1).

The spasms grew stronger by the minute, and they affected many muscles in my body. There was a wild and strange intensity, with an unusual type and level of sensuality. Possibly because I possessed a small degree of discernment, or because I have not been a seeker of pleasure, this was not enjoyable to me. I began to feel frightened and out of control. Something was happening *to* me, rather than *with* my consent. I did not know how to stop these movements, which was unprecedented in my life.

Despite my desire for this to stop, I did not consider at that moment that it could be from Satan. The reason I could not consider this is that my theology of Satan precluded this possibility. My spiritual reasoning was as follows: Since I had not sinned or opened any door to Satan through my thoughts or behavior, I believed that he would not have permission to manipulate my body against my will. Sin opens a legal door to the enemy, and I had not opened this door. How could my body move against my will, with no ability to stop it? This was out of my range of understanding.

I was also concerned that the experience had a sensual quality; however, there was no involvement of the usual zones nor did I sense an evil presence, apart from fear. I wondered if this event might be an expression of the Bridegroom's love for His Bride, although in perfect hindsight, I now realize that fear and unwelcome manifestations would never be part of our Lord Yeshua's gentle and respectful love. It is much easier to discern this event in hindsight, and the telling of the story carries helpful information that did not accompany the original experience. The truth is more evident now than during the actual experience at the time. I am recounting the events with all the benefits of wisdom and discernment given to me as a result of this trial.

As strange and naïve as this might seem, I did not connect this event to the warning I had received from the Lord three days earlier. My limited understanding of the word "temptation" did not include what was happening to me at that moment. Nothing like this had ever happened to me in all my life, and I was not only innocent, but also ignorant of evil's devices until the test was over.

But the wisdom that comes from heaven is first of all pure; then peace-loving, considerate, submissive, full of mercy and good fruit, impartial and sincere (James 3:17).

This shocking event lasted close to an hour and exhausted me. When my roommate Katya woke up, it mysteriously stopped, and I tried to share with her what had happened to me. Despite the fact that she was a mature believer, with some background in spiritual warfare, she also was not ready to discern this unusual experience. I got up, and we prepared for a long day of meetings.

All day Wednesday, we participated in the repentance meetings, and I was filled with His Spirit continually. At 4:00 p.m., we went back to the hotel to rest before the evening meeting. I was very tired and just wanted to rest. The minute I lay down, and my roommate had fallen asleep, the spasms started again; I was dismayed and frightened. I told the Lord I did not want this manifestation (thinking it was from Him), but they just continued. I reasoned that the Lord would not do something against my will, so I started to say, "If this is not from the Lord God, I reject it, in Jesus' Name," but the spasms did not stop. This confused me more.

I continued to test what was happening, and what might make it stop. I started to recite Psalm 23. The moment I began, it stopped! Then I thought, "Perhaps this is not of God, since His Word caused it to stop immediately (Eph. 6:17). After reciting this Psalm again, a knock came on my hotel door, and one of the other intercessors was inviting me to take a walk outside. As exhausted as I was, it was a relief to be able to leave the hotel room and get away from the situation.

After the evening meeting, we got to bed very late, almost midnight. The minute I lay down and my roommate was asleep, it started again. I was now certain that this was an attack, and it was not from God, but I was still confused. My confusion was this: I knew that the Holy Spirit lived within me. I knew that Satan most certainly did not live within me. Therefore, how could Satan make my body move against my will when he does not live in me? Surely, only God could move my body against my free will, and yet God is gentle and respectful; if I told Him to stop, surely He would stop. Such was my reasoning.

Since Psalm 23 had worked in stopping the afternoon attack, I started to recite it again but this time, it didn't work. Therefore, scriptural formulas are not the answer. Then I started to recite Matthew 6:9-13, and it instantly stopped at the first word! I recited the Lord's Prayer four more times just to make sure, and I slept peacefully through the rest of the night. Let the reader be patient with me, but I still had not comprehended the bigger picture of what was happening.

On Thursday, we participated in the conference all day and returned to the hotel for an afternoon rest. Of course, the minute I hit the bed, it started again. Enough, already! What I could not seem to grasp on my own, the merciful Holy Spirit finally told me outright: *"It's the bed."* I jumped out of bed, horrified. I got into Katya's bed and told her what was happening. As I lay in her peaceful bed, my body was blissfully still, and I finally knew that the origin of this manifestation was not from inside my own body but from an outside source. This was the key I had been missing since the day before, when this phenomenon had begun on Wednesday morning.

While I rested in both shock and relief, Katya knelt down by my hateful bed and cast the demon out. She felt some resistance, and then it left, never to return. After several minutes, I worked up all my courage and got back into my bed to test the situation. I was free and peaceful for the remainder of the trip.

One last step that I took to bring this disturbing saga to an end was to go before the Lord and fully renounce and cleanse myself from this damaging experience. I knelt down and told the Lord that I fully rejected and renounced this manifestation and that I never wanted to feel anything of this sort again. I prayed for His blood to cleanse me and for His Spirit to restore my mind, body and spirit from any defilement that had come as a result of this test.

Looking back on this, it is clear that we should have done a spiritual cleansing of the room and the bed when we first checked in. This is an important precaution all believers should take when checking into a room. Many wicked things take place in hotel rooms, and there may be residual spirits which can influence the atmosphere in the room, even if Christians are staying there. In my case, it was an extreme case of "infestation" by a demon on assignment, as will be demonstrated in the following section.

Some may be wondering, "How was this a case of 'temptation'? Doesn't 'temptation' mean that we have a choice as to whether to sin or not? In this situation, I was assaulted without any choice in the matter. I wondered about this myself.

To the best of my understanding, the temptation was this: I was given the opportunity to experience sensual pleasure of a type and level previously unknown to me. It was a very real option for me to agree to participate in this pleasure. If I was not sure whether it was of God, I could have continued to tell myself that it was of God, so that I could feel free to indulge in this corruptive adventure. This would have been viewed by heaven as a betrayal of my covenant with God, and I would have chosen sensuality over the pure and holy love of God. His love is gentle and full of tender respect for our wishes and our agreement with Him. The Lord would never force Himself on anyone who did not want Him. This counterfeit experience was forceful, and even when I wanted it to stop, it had no respect for my wishes. It was mocking me and driving me to a place I did not wish to go. Passivity was not an option; if I did not actively reject it, I would have been worshiping Satan.

Even though I was innocent, Satan was given permission by God to do this to me in order to test my integrity, as well as my discernment. The enemy wanted to entice me, which would have caused the Lord grief and shame if I were to fail the test. Satan wanted to show the Lord that I did not love Him and that I would choose pleasure over Him.

Despite my lack of discernment in the first appearance of this manifestation (of which I am not proud), I resisted this sensual experience to the best of my ability. Thus, in the Lord's eyes, I did not fail this test. I give Him honor and thanks for helping me to overcome this unexpected and confusing form of trial.

The Lord was kind and gracious to warn me ahead of time; He permitted this test to happen, but He also made a way of escape for me so that I could come through this awful test without suffering shame and remorse. Peter tells us that our faith will be tested with fire, even as gold is refined, in order that our faith will be proved genuine. (1Pet. 1:7)

> *No temptation has seized you except what is common to man. And God is faithful; he will not let you be tempted beyond what you can bear. But when you are tempted, he will also provide a way out so that you can stand up under it* (1 Co. 10:13).

The Terror Test

We flew home from Birmingham on Saturday. The flight home was very long, and we were delayed, due to weather problems. After settling in with my family and unpacking, I got to bed rather late that night and was exhausted. The following experience happened at 1:00 a.m. while I was sleeping peacefully.

Suddenly, I was jolted awake by a sensation of being freezing cold. At the same time, a thick and dreadful terror was all around me, which caused me to quiver violently. I was unable to move or speak, so great was the level of power upon me.

Like most people, I have known fear. I have been in serious car accidents and have suffered the phobia of cockroaches described in the Israel chapter. I was once inches away from being assaulted on my college campus, and the fear I felt then was significant. But there is no vocabulary sufficient to describe the formidable, tangible terror I felt that night. It seemed alive. I pray I never feel anything like it again as long as I live.

As with the previous test, it is much easier to discern this event in hindsight, and the telling of the story carries helpful information that did not accompany the original experience. It may seem obvious now that this fear could only have come from Satan. However, at that moment, awakened out of a deep sleep, I genuinely believed this was the "Spirit of the fear of the Lord," named in Isaiah 11:1-3. There are three passages in the Book of Revelation which state that there are seven spirits of God (Rev 1:4, 4:5 and 5:5).

Then I saw a Lamb, looking as if it had been slain, standing in the center of the throne, encircled by the four living creatures and the elders. He had seven horns and seven eyes, which are the seven spirits of God sent out into all the earth (Rev. 5:6).

Isaiah lists these seven spirits as belonging to the Branch that will spring up from Jesse's roots, who is Messiah Yeshua. Jesse was the father of King David, and Yeshua is the righteous Branch from the Davidic lineage (also see the Messiah as "the Branch" in Isaiah 4:2).

The Spirit of the LORD will rest on him; the Spirit of wisdom and of under-standing, the Spirit of counsel and of power, the Spirit of knowledge and of the fear of the LORD; and he will delight in the fear of the LORD (Isa. 11:2-3).

I was familiar with several passages of Scripture, in which our patriarchs felt a great fear in God's Presence. When Abraham was about to receive the covenant of the Land of Israel, Genesis 15 records that "a thick and dread dark-ness" came over him. I knew that at Mount Sinai, a great terror came over the people when God descended to the mountain. Not only did the people tremble, but the mountain trembled as well. When Daniel saw a mighty angel, he fell on his face trembling and said that he could not even breathe.

My ancestors had felt the fear of the Lord at Mt. Sinai, and I believed He was teaching me what it meant to know the "fear of the Lord." To me, this was a fully biblical aspect of God, and it did not occur to me that Satan was in my bedroom, terrifying me with his tremendous power.

This fearful visitation did not remain at the same high level constantly, but ebbed and flowed. When it would fade slightly, I was able to speak; when it was at its most dreadful, I was virtually paralyzed. After lying in these waves of dread for almost half an hour, I began to think, by the prompting of His Spirit, "What if this is not God?"

During an interval while I was able to speak, I said, "If this fear is from God, give me the Spirit test" (1 John 4:2-3). I wanted to hear it clearly say that "Jesus Christ has come in the flesh," according to this biblical test of discernment. After a slight hesitation, an unpleasant voice answered me in a somewhat snarling tone, "Jesus Christ has come in the fle...ss..." The last word trailed off without perfect clarity, but it managed to say the rest of the sentence. I thought the tone sounded too angry to be God, but I was very tired and wondered if perhaps God might be angry. Nevertheless, I was ready to do business.

It was time to rebuke it. First, I said, "If this fear is not from the Lord God, I reject it and send it away, in Jesus' name." This did not remove it, and I tried one other similar phrase, without success. It was very hard for me to find the strength to speak, let alone use a strong and commanding tone with this presence. I mustered all my resolve, and finally I spoke with the authority that was needed. In a seriously forceful tone, I used the phrase, "The Lord rebuke you!" (Jude 9) It instantly lifted off me, pulling back at high speed.

The atmosphere around me was replaced instantly with a visitation of God's true glory. First I saw the clear blue heavens full of clouds; then a cross appeared in the clouds; then Yeshua was hanging on the cross with a light from heaven shining down on Him like a spotlight; then I heard many voices say "Jesus Christ has come in the flesh" in a clear, sweet, almost musical tone. They said this phrase freely and happily, in stark contrast to the ugly snarl I had just heard a minute before. Then I lay in His true glory for a long time, which helped me to recover from the horrible fear which I had thought was God.

While I was in the glory, the Lord showed me in a vision the demon which had been in my bed in Birmingham. I was observing this hideous creature from a distance, and he could not see me. He was standing at the check-in counter at the hotel in Birmingham, as if he were a normal human guest checking in. His head was large, bald and ugly. His top half looked like a large, bare-chested human man, bulky, like a wrestler. His lower half was massive and reptilian, with a long tail. It was quite an education for me, to say the least.

I could not bear to contemplate such an evil and repulsive being occupying my bed, let alone the disgust and remorse I would suffer if I had given it any satisfaction. If believers could see the unseen demonic powers that derive gratification from making God's people fall into the snare of sin, they would not willfully indulge in secret sins, thinking they will ask for forgiveness later. What sacrifice will be left for their continual and deliberate sins? (Heb. 10:26-27)

Lessons Learned

As in the case of the first test, I wondered, *What makes this experience a temptation? What choices did I have in this matter?* If I had continued to stay captive to the overpowering fear and had treated the presence as I would treat God Himself, I would have been worshiping Satan. To stay in the fearful presence, trembling and helpless, was to show it respect, awe and reverence. It is fitting for a believer to submit to God when He overshadows him with great power, but to submit to the enemy is idolatrous worship. Even if I did not realize it was Satan, I would still be showing him awe and respect, in place of God. By the Lord's grace and prompting, I was able to come to my senses, test the spirits, and cast the evil counterfeit out of my presence. I give the Lord Yeshua praise for helping me once again in my weakness.

These two different tests happened within the span of one week, the week between the Feasts of Rosh Hashannah and Yom Kippur. It was precisely twelve years since the true glory visitation I described in Chapter 3. These tests both came as counterfeit experiences of God's power and glory. The first one imitated the pleasure of being in God's glory. The second one imitated the fear of being in God's glory. In both cases, I was misled into believing the presence I was feeling was from the Lord. In both cases, I needed to discern correctly and then cast it out with authority.

These two tests came with a high level of power, to the extent that I thought only God Himself could be responsible for such compelling, supernatural manifestations. Both were expressions of the enemy's hatred for me and for all who love the Lord wholeheartedly. Neither counterfeit experience reflected God's love, purity, kindness, gentleness, or shalom. May I discern more quickly and act immediately in the future. Amen.

All who love the Lord will be tested in various ways, in order to sharpen their discernment, exercise their authority, strengthen their character and prove their resolve. It is written in Chronicles that the Lord "withdrew from Hezekiah, to test everything that was in his heart."

The Warning of Balaam

Although this is a most unpleasant subject, the Lord has shown me repeatedly, since these incidents, that one of Satan's most devastating attacks on the people of God in these last days will be sexual immorality. It will be unleashed in a variety of forms, some quite unexpected; the Lord has permitted me to undergo several more attacks and tests in this area, in diverse manifestations. In each case, He taught me the importance of calling on the name of the Lord immediately, and forcefully rebuking this thing before it achieves its goals, which are the ruin, exploitation and shame of God's precious children. Ignorance or passivity will not be an acceptable excuse in the day that we give an account.

With eyes full of adultery, they never stop sinning; they seduce the unstable; they are experts in greed, an accursed brood! They have left the straight way and wandered off to follow the way of Balaam, son of Beor, who loved the wages of wickedness... For they mouth empty, boastful words and by appealing to the lustful desires of sinful human nature, they entice people who are just escaping from those who live in error. They promise them freedom, while they themselves are slaves of depravity—for a man is a slave to whatever has mastered him (2 Pet. 2:14-15, 18-19).

Nevertheless, I have a few things against you. You have people there who hold to the teaching of Balaam, who taught Balak to entice the Israelites to sin by eating food sacrificed to idols and by committing sexual immorality (Rev. 2:14).

The false prophet Balaam attempted to curse Israel for money. When the Lord prevented him from doing so, he employed a different strategy, which was even more destructive. He taught the Moabite king, Balak, how to seduce the Israelite men. Once Satan had successfully enticed them, they were out from under God's divine protection and easy prey for the adversary.

Why is this Gentile false prophet Balaam mentioned three times in the New Testament and many times in the Old Testament? It is because this very strategy will be Satan's preferred weapon against the Church. An onslaught of temptation, seduction, defilement and molestation will be unleashed against us, precisely as Balaam and Balak employed these tools to destroy Israel.

Outside [the gates of the city] are the dogs, those who practice magic arts, the sexually immoral, the idolaters and everyone who loves and practices falsehood (Rev. 22:15).

I recently had a nasty dream about a wicked seducer and imposter, who was pretending to be a Christian; the other character was a kindly "mature" woman who was supposed to be mentoring me, but she herself was seduced later in the dream. Early in this dream, the woman was giving me counsel, which I knew was not what I needed and only partially correct, but I listened to her out of respect and courtesy.

After the scene had changed, I reached out to talk to the woman, but in the place where she had been, the seducer appeared, and I could no longer find the woman. I heard a male voice whispering in my ear, and he was attempting to entice me. This man had taken the name of a New Testament figure and was seemingly a believer. I was using human reasoning, biblical arguments, and my own physical strength to resist him, but these human attempts did not discourage him.

At one point in his advances, the woman appeared again; before I could ask her to help me get away from him, I realized from her appearance that she had already been seduced by him! I asked her incredulously why she had done this, but she smiled reassuringly that all was well. She offered me no help to escape, but assured me that it would be "good" to be with him, and I needn't worry.

For some reason, I called upon the woman's name to help me escape from him, rather than calling on the name of the Lord. When the Lord asked me the next morning why I did not call upon His name, I could only answer that in this dream, it did not occur to me. I thought the woman would protect me. Before the dream ended, I realized that this man would not honor my resistance or my wishes and would ruin me anyway. A feeling of doom came over me. I awoke as a merciful escape from him, but I was both frightened and ashamed. Why had I not thought to call out the Lord Jesus' name while I still could?

The Lord then spoke to me about the danger of passivity, and of not calling out upon His name. He reminded me that, in the Birmingham experience, when I rejected the spirit that was manipulating my body, even using the phrase "in Jesus' name," it did not stop. It only stopped when I spoke the Word of God aloud. In the evil "fear" visitation, the evil presence did not depart until I forcefully said, "The Lord rebuke you!"

The Lord explained that when it was "I" who was rejecting the evil one, it did not work. There is a difference between using the phrase "in Jesus' name" as a formula for deliverance, and actually rebuking the evil one in the name, agreement and authority of the Lord's command.

This is difficult to explain, but when we command, He commands, if we are in union with Him and His authority reigns in us. If we only use His name as an appendage to our weak version of resistance, the more powerful evil spirits do not need to obey us, if I have understood this correctly. Only the Lord Himself could rebuke and banish this unusual and powerful evil spirit. He explained that in both of the previous attacks, as well as the dream about the seducer, only calling upon His name aloud would be effectual.

> Even the archangel Michael, when he was disputing with the devil about the body of Moses, did not dare to bring a slanderous accusation against him, but said, "The Lord rebuke you!" (Jude 9)

In the Birmingham experience, when I quoted Psalm 23 the first time, the attack stopped. This was because I was using the Word of God as a weapon of war. The second time I quoted the identical Psalm, it did not work. The reason was this: I was using a "tried and true" formula, which would only wield power to the extent that it was a sincere weapon from my heart, coming out of my mouth. When I began to quote the Lord's Prayer, the attack stopped because I was bringing to bear a fresh Scripture with the authority of the Word used as a weapon, rather than a remedy. I hope I have conveyed this distinction clearly to the reader, as it is vital to grasp in the battle that we face.

The Lord told me that the Word of God in my mouth was the only weapon that would prevail in the unprecedented and powerful onslaught that is about to be unleashed on His people. If I remained silent, and tried to deal with it privately, I would be lost. If I hesitated, it would be too late. He continued: *"If you keep his secret, he will end up having you. Your human strength and resistance will not work anymore. My enemy is coming to My people now with a strong spirit of seduction. It is very strong and deceiving, and those who resist him in their own strength will be seduced or raped. That is why quoting My Word was the only thing that stopped his assaults in Birmingham."*

Sometimes this enticement will be of a physical nature, and other times, it will involve a spiritual and idolatrous deception which the Lord Jesus describes in Matthew 24. The Bible teaches that idolatry, sexual immorality and adultery are enticements which separate the Lord from His people, due to His holiness and purity. The Lord continued to teach me that I must call out His name at the first moment that the enticement or attack begins, and should not rely on my own arguments. If I wait to call upon the Lord until I am overpowered, it will be too late because the evil one will silence me, and the sword of the Word will not be able to come out of my mouth. During the "terror visitation," the enemy's power was so great I could not speak. The Lord reminded me, as He did the Philadelphian church in Revelation, that I "have little power."

The Lord also explained that the woman in the dream represented the Church. She was seemingly older and wiser, but I had sensed in my spirit that the counsel she was giving me was not completely right. It had elements of truth in it, but something was amiss. Perhaps I had weakened my spirit or my resistance early in the dream by politely listening to her teaching, which I knew was not fully biblical.

By the time I called out to her to help me, she had already been seduced, and she actually attempted to weaken my resolve when I asked for her help. He said, *"This is what the church will do. She will be seduced, and then she will not lift a finger to help others who are being seduced or overpowered, but will even entice them to participate so that she herself will feel less shame."*

Some might object to this troubling statement, concerning the seduction of the "church" in the last days. They might argue, "How can the Bride of Messiah be seduced? Is she a Bride or a harlot?"

To the best of my understanding, when the Lord used the word "the church" in the interpretation of the woman, He was not referring to the true Bride of Messiah, who has made herself spotless and ready for His appearing. He was referring to a significant segment of the professing church which is not walking in complete holiness and purity before Him now; therefore, they will be easy prey to the deceptive and seducing spirit that will come. Yeshua said in Matthew 24, that the deception at the end will be so enticing that even the very elect of God would be deceived, if that were possible.

We already see enormous and grievous compromise in the standards and purity of the so-called church. In both the evangelical and charismatic church, sexual sins of every variety are occurring before His face. The Lord's heart is broken by the immorality and adultery within His church, and among the leaders of His people. How many times must He suffer and hang on the cross to save His church from continual and willful sin? (Heb. 6:4-6) This is apostasy!

Yeshua then asked me to promise Him that in whatever form the next manifestation of seduction comes, I will respond immediately by calling out upon His name. He told me it would be stronger than the seducing spirit I felt in the dream and would be a matter of life and death. I gave Him my sacred promise, and may His grace enable me to keep it. Amen.

So, if you think you are standing firm, be careful that you don't fall! No temptation has seized you except what is common to man. And God is faithful; he will not let you be tempted beyond what you can bear. But when you are tempted, he will also provide a way out so that you can stand up under it (1 Co. 10:12-13).

CHAPTER 5

SECRETS OF INTIMATE FRIENDSHIP

After the fall feasts of 2005, the next three months were a dry and difficult period. As I waited on the Lord, I would often feel empty and unfulfilled at the end of the session. There were some occasions when I received a visitation from Him; but overall, I grew sad and frustrated. However, there was one particular encounter which contained a very important key for the lives of all true believers.

Nailed With Him

On the Shabbat morning of December 24th, I was waiting on the Lord, and I sensed Him kneeling at my feet. I tried to dismiss this "picture" as wrong, since He is my Lord and I worship Him. However, I tried to be open to what He was showing me.

He was kneeling with a basin of water at my feet, and He began to wash them. I wanted to protest, but I remembered what He had told Peter: "Unless you let Me wash your feet, you have no part with Me." Not wanting to be rebuked, I allowed Him to show this kindness to me, while I kissed the top of His sweet head. He said nothing but was busy with His act of service. He then carefully dried my feet with a big towel and arranged my feet on the floor.

The Lord then took out the longest nail I have ever seen, and in a matter-of-fact way, began to pound it into my right foot with a large mallet. I was appalled, although there was no physical pain. Then he took another nail and drove it through my left foot. (I trust it is understood that this was a spiritual act, without any physical piercing taking place.) I wondered why the Lord would do such an unkind thing, after showing me such kindness. Yeshua then told me to hold out my hands, which I did; He drove a nail through each of them as well. Then I sat there, confused and troubled. The Lord then spoke to me: *"Don't you understand what I've done to you? You have been crucified with Me. It is I who live through you, and you do not have your own will, plans or agenda. Will you follow Me to death?"*

I said, "Yes," and I knew this was a living parable of Galatians 2:20. At that time, I had no information about my physical death, except for the experience of my heart stopping in 2003 (documented in Chapter 4). I now know He was preparing me for more revelation in the near future.

Ask Him What He Desires

Despite a few encouraging experiences, I grew discouraged in my regular "waiting" times, as so many seemed uneventful. By the end of January 2006, I was too dry and hopeless to sit in my chair for an hour, and walk away empty. Often, I would get up after about half an hour and say sadly, "I'm sorry, Lord. I just can't do this."

I did not know why this was happening. Part of me thought that the Lord was sovereignly choosing to be distant from me, in order to test my faith and perseverance. Another part of me thought that He would not do that, after all we had been through in the glory department. I knew Him to be a kind and loving God, who was eager to spend intimate time with His children, so why were my times of waiting so lonely and unsatisfying? I began to sense that He was not deliberately frustrating me, but rather that something was missing. There must be some ingredient I was lacking, which would refresh and restore my relationship with Him.

During the last week in January, I called my best friend and prayer partner, and as soon as she picked up the phone, I burst into tears. She was surprised and concerned.

"What's wrong, Jill?"

"I'm so depressed," I sobbed. "He doesn't come to me anymore."

"I'm going to ask Him to give me a Word for you, honey."

"Thank you, Katya."

A friend who will go before the Lord and seek Him for a word of encouragement on my behalf...how can anyone put a value on that kind of gift? I have no words for my gratitude to this faithful woman who has brought me numerous life-changing words from our Father's heart.

I received the following word from her the next day; I urge each reader to carefully consider this word as pertaining not to me alone, but to each one of the Lord's children who seeks greater intimacy with Him. I believe that the reason the Lord wants this complete word presented in this book, is to benefit each reader, and to greatly accelerate each one's intimate friendship with Him:

Ask Me what I desire. Do I desire to just sit in your presence? Do I desire that you sing to Me? Do I desire that you worship before Me? Do I desire that you lay at My altar and offer yourself and nothing else? Do I desire that you share your happiness and excited chatter with Me? I love all of you, not just a discipline that you can do.

Sometimes I really do desire that you sit completely still and quiet before Me and nothing else, but other times, I desire to hear your heart. Come to Me as you are.

I desire much, but it cannot be measured by anything you can do or give. It is measured by how you know Me. As you come to Me as you are, I come to know you! I desire to know you and your heart. What do you treasure about Me? What does your heart feel about Me? Do you remember how you first came to Me? Do you treasure our relationship? Count the ways of our times together. How have I blessed you? Have you treasured in your heart our precious relationship? Am I your best friend? Am I your lover, your husband, your King? Recount and remember our times together. When My people remember what I've done to deliver them, they light candles, they read My Word, but are they treasuring in their hearts their own personal deliverance? I know that you do, My daughter.

I want more of your heart, My love. I seek and desire your lovely thoughts of Me, and your memories in thankfulness and treasuring our relationship together.

I know that this is a newer area, since your own earthly father and husband have not understood treasuring and remembering precious moments spent together, and they have not recounted them with you. I want you to remember what we have together, through many precious memories, and then we can seek more together. Come with a full heart, as you have in the past, and then after we have spent a wonderful time looking through our memory book together, let's make plans for the future. I am *always* there, so even while you are thinking, remembering, planning, I am listening. So then with your memories, joys, sorrows and thankful heart, come.

In the same way that you have your coffee time with your daughter, I just want a coffee time with My daughter, to laugh, cry, talk or just sit together. It is *so* precious to Me. Is it precious to you? I know it is. Just come. Sometimes there is much you and your daughter share, other times it's a little more quiet, but your time together is treasured. Come to Me with the treasures of your heart, mind and soul…I am waiting for you.

Come to Me with more pleasure than you do your most precious and trusted friends. I am jealous for you, My daughter. I don't ask for anything from you, just come and know you are My most treasured one. Come knowing My gaze is on you, My dove, My love.

Read Song of Songs and hear how much I love you, and desire your heart. Don't limit yourself, My daughter, to one way of coming to Me. I desire all of you, and one man's way of hearing Me may not be how I speak to you, and how you hear Me.

Let's discover our own relationship, let's discover how you hear Me, and how we relate together. It is unique, like you are unique, like a snowflake. Remember, you can do what others do, but it still may not enhance our unique personal relationship. I desire My real daughter, not a replica of another.

This amazing word ignited my motivation to pour out all my thoughts, love, treasures, memories, thankfulness, worship, tears, laughter, disappointments, regrets, concerns and excited chatter before His face. From this moment on, I began to add a great deal of my heart's content to the quietness of waiting. I did not forsake the silent discipline, but I spent a great deal more time with words and acts of intense worship and transparent verbal expressions to Him. This word is really the key to an intimate relationship with the Lord. Through our voluntary sharing of everything in our heart, He comes to know us.

I began to obey this Word by reviewing my life and memories with Him. I would just begin recounting stories and situations in which I had seen His help and deliverance. He wanted to hear me tell Him my story; it is my life's testimony. Some of these memories were presented here in this book of my testimony, which He is pleased for me to share with others.

After obeying this prophetic word, I found that during February and March, I was very blessed to receive a number of visitations of His Presence, several taking place during the night with great power from the Lord. One of them was followed by a demonic attack. It is not necessary to detail these experiences; it is more important to press on to the next chapter in our relationship, which is the true purpose of this writing.

My waiting times improved greatly during this period of preparation, after pouring out more of my heart to Him as Katya's word instructed me. I have deliberately included the above prophetic word in its entirety, because I know the Lord wants to enlarge many of His people through it. He will use this word to energize and refresh many of His children's devotional times with Him, which will lead to a rapid growth in their intimacy with our precious Lord Jesus. He desires to do these marvelous things with each one who loves Him wholeheartedly. His goodness is inexhaustible.

I believe with all my heart that this generous prophetic word I received from Katya was not only for my benefit, but for all of the Lord's children. Our Savior has a way of making each one of us feel that we are the most treasured one in the universe, but He has millions of "most treasured ones"! All who seek Him will find Him; all who honor Him, He will honor! All who worship Him according to His desires and not our own preferences will reap a harvest of His delight and joy!

The Lord deals righteously with each of us, and any who will put into practice the principles outlined in this awesome word of what He desires, will reap the wonderful benefits and rewards that I have reaped, even greater rewards!

> *The man who thinks he knows something does not yet know as he ought to know. But the man who loves God is known by God* (1 Co. 8:2-3).

> *Since ancient times no one has heard, no ear has perceived, no eye has seen any God besides you, who acts on behalf of those who wait for him"* (Is. 64:4).

CHAPTER 6

THREE DAY ENCOUNTER

On March 24, 2006, the Lord gave Katya a detailed prophetic word for me, which was unexpected. He requested that I set aside the first three days of any week of my choosing and shut myself away with Him in my room. He preferred that I accomplish this before Passover, although it was not a requirement. I had extensive ministry responsibilities during the Passover period, and it would benefit me to have had this time of consecration before this ministry would take place.

This word contained specific instructions about my conduct during the period of seclusion. I was to prepare my family, business contacts, ministries and friends ahead of time, so that there would be no contact with anyone. I needed to clean my room, change the bedding, and make some furniture adjustments to create the needed environment. The Lord also wanted me to place objects around the room that had special meaning to me in my history with Him—memorials of His faithfulness.

I was to fast on "Yahveh's Bread" for three days before the period of seclusion began, but was permitted to bring a cooler of food up to the room in order to eat simple meals with Yeshua during the seclusion. The Lord instructed me to worship Him without recorded music; there would be no musical or teaching CDs or tapes. I was to light candles at sunset and take communion with Him at the times He would show me. I was not to wear shoes and was to wear fresh pajamas each night. Instructions were also given regarding when to shower, and when to wear the tallit. The extreme care taken in matters of hygiene, holiness and purity reminded me of the Levitical regulations for priests who minister before His holy presence.

Most importantly, this word instructed me to use this precious time to bring the Lord all the offerings of my heart. I was to give Him all of my thanks, worship, praise, prayers, devotion, private thoughts, opinions, disappointments and even anger. This was not a time to hold back from Him anything that was in my heart, whether good or bad. The Lord would be watching and listening intently to see if I would be utterly transparent before Him. Obeying this particular instruction proved to be of immeasurable benefit to my eternal destiny. As the end of this chapter will demonstrate, the rewards from God for utter transparency and complete honesty are beyond all the happiness, wealth and rewards of this world's system.

I received this word with great joy and anticipation. My spirit leapt to think that He would grant me three days alone with Him, free from all the normal distractions. I looked at my calendar and immediately identified the only possible block of days before Passover: I would begin at sunset on Saturday, April 1st and would be released on Tuesday, April 4th at sunset. It took me five days to complete the significant preparations for these three days. On the appointed Shabbat, I kissed my family goodbye before sunset, went upstairs and shut the door. I was formally released by Yeshua at one hour before the sunset on the third day.

The emotions that filled my heart in the days leading up to this unique three-day "date" with the Lord Yeshua are hard to describe. With nervous anticipation, I wondered what would happen to me. There was a small element of fear, which included the fear of claustrophobia and boredom, as well as some slight mistrust of His faithfulness to be "readily available" to me. What if I couldn't think of anything to do or say to Him, or ran out of prayers after the first day? Sometimes, I couldn't even pray for more than fifteen minutes! But the greatest fear was that I had no concept of what He would do with me, best characterized by, "What am I getting myself into?"

In earlier centuries, some parents thought they were doing their virgin daughters a favor by keeping them "innocent" of the facts of life; they deliberately did not tell them what to expect on their wedding night. Many of these sheltered creatures knew nothing about the most basic elements of human sexuality and went trembling into the wedding night with a great fear of the unknown. Sometimes, this initial fear damaged the couple's future relationship.

This feeling of a fluttering bird or a nervous and sheltered bride is the closest analogy I can use to describe the strange combination of joy, fear and anticipation I felt, approaching my three days. As I looked around my room, and surveyed all the objects and photographs that depicted the Lord's reality in my life and His miraculous answers to prayers, I felt that my bedroom was a clean, holy and respectful environment in which to invite the most welcome "guest" one could ever hope to receive.

The First Day

At sunset, I showered and anointed myself with spikenard oil, lit the candles, and consecrated our appointed time in prayer as the sky drew dark. I spent time singing to the Lord spontaneous melodies and words of praise in English and Hebrew, and talking to Him about His faithfulness to me, despite my wretched failures over the years. I knelt in prayer to intercede for my family, asking Yeshua to take care of their needs while I was away. I sang, without accompaniment, four or five worship songs that I knew, and danced before Him. Before going to bed, I blew out the candles and read the Scriptures.

I was wakeful during most of that first night. When I arose in the morning, I played my guitar and worshiped the Lord. I sang quite a few Messianic Hebrew songs, many taken directly from the Psalms. I also sang these same songs in English, to get the words deeper into my spirit. I was unusually aware that He was with me at all times and was listening intently to everything I would offer Him that day. I never allowed myself to drift off in thought or daydream, but rather stayed very connected to what Yeshua was observing.

I moved to a chair which my husband had kindly moved into the bedroom for my three days, and read aloud Psalms 103, 104 and 105. I read them as sincere prayers from my own heart, and it was awesome how the words were alive to me. Then I prayed for my family again. Finally, at about 8:30, it was time for coffee with Yeshua!

When I had first received instructions about these three days, I had sadly assumed the Lord would not want me to have my morning coffee, due to the consecration of this time. I had told Him I would like my coffee, but I wasn't whining about it. Several days before I began, Katya went to a Christian bookstore to surprise me with anointing oils; while she was driving there, the Holy Spirit told her that I could have my coffee.

When she got to the store, she saw a blue coffee mug with a Scripture on it that was perfect for me. Despite the fact that I own many coffee mugs, this special time required a new cup that had never been used for ordinary purposes. I was overjoyed to receive His permission and my new cup. To this day, this particular cup is precious to me, and only used for "coffee talks" with my precious Yeshua!

As I slowly sipped my coffee that Sunday morning, we conversed as dear friends. I had never experienced a leisurely conversation with the Lord Jesus with my eyes open, in which I could "hear" Him responding to everything I said, as a normal friend would respond. Though I could not see Him, it was real and satisfying. During many of our talks that would take place after that time, I could sense Him in the room, and at other times, I saw Him rather clearly with the eyes of my heart.

This newly discovered form of fellowship with Him would become the foundation of a discipline of regular appointments called "coffee talks." These talks, as they have matured over time, are indeed intimate and comforting; however, they are also complex, penetrating and far less casual than they might appear on the surface. There is nothing casual about our Lord Yeshua, nor is it possible for me to be completely comfortable in His presence. (A detailed description of the true atmosphere of a coffee talk, and some of the difficulties I encountered in pursuing them, is found in Chapter 8.)

I would think that a number of the Lord's children are already enjoying these or other types of conversations with Him, and I am not suggesting that I have discovered a new planet. For me, however, it opened up a new universe of intimacy with Him, which has greatly accelerated every level of my walk, relationships, integrity and good fruits. Throughout the Gospel accounts, Yeshua spent time in intimate fellowship with His disciples, often over meals. I believe that "coffee talks" are truly a continuation of the pattern of our Lord's close relationships with His friends, His *y'didim*.

Behold the Banana

I was eating half a banana as we conversed, and He began to show me the wonder of the banana. He allowed me to slowly savor, for the first time, the amazing flavor and texture of the banana. He showed me the metaphor of His perfect timing for the ripening of all things. Within the tough and protective skin, He had placed the chemicals needed to ripen the fruit. When the skin is green, the fruit is hard and tasteless, and it would be a waste to eat it early. Then it becomes yellow, and a few days later, begins to develop black spots. This signifies the maximum flavor and sweetness. Then when the perfect moment has passed, it gets blacker and blacker, and the fruit becomes soft and eventually liquefies into a repulsive condition.

All of His redemptive plans, including the birth and return of Yeshua, have to come in "the fullness of time." In fulfilling His plans for our lives, we must be in step with His timing. If we move too early, the plans are "unripe." If too late, they have decayed and their optimum fulfillment is past.

"Losing His Presence"

After coffee, I knelt for intercessory prayer. Then I sat in my rocking chair and combined several disciplines. I spoke words of devotion and waited on the Lord, but I also spent time reviewing His faithfulness in my life. According to the prophetic word presented in the last chapter, my Lord desired that I go over my memories with Him. I spent about an hour recounting all that He had done in my children's lives since we had returned from Israel. There were so many kinds of help and deliverance I had forgotten; taking the time to retell our story is very valuable to Him, because it shows Him we remember His acts of kindness to us in our very personal and unique history.

I then had a small lunch, and conversed with Him for almost an hour, similar to the relaxed conversation we had in the morning. Each meal and coffee time for the remainder of the three days was like this: intimate, two-way conversation flowed, and I was amazed at the joy of knowing Him as a friend for the first time in thirty-three years.

During the afternoon hours, I journalled the events of the morning and His revelations of the afternoon. This included asking Him many questions on my heart. I asked Him for revelation about His end-time purposes in my life, financial offerings He wished me to make over the coming year, conferences I should attend, the children's destinies, my teaching ministry, and church-related matters. The Lord Yeshua answered almost all of my questions. When I asked Him about my destiny, I did not know what I was asking. He answered that question on the second day, but had I known what He would show me, I wonder if I would have had the courage to ask.

In the middle of that first afternoon, I "lost" His presence. The Lord just seemed not to be in the room anymore. I had to make a determined effort not to become discouraged. I wondered why I felt so alone. Would the whole three days be like this? I didn't think I could go on without any evidence of His companionship.

I read some Scripture, and then took Communion. I hoped that this act would restore the sense of the Lord's presence to me, but it did not. I had a small meal, lit the evening candles, and spent the next few hours worshipping Him. I sang my favorite Hebrew Psalms, which filled me with hope that I would be aware of His presence again. Since I needed to hear from the Lord in the morning, the last song I sang before bed was "*Hashmieni*" (Let Me Hear), taken from Psalm 143:

Let the morning bring me word of your unfailing love, for I have put my trust in you. Show me the way I should go, for to you I lift up my soul. Rescue me from my enemies, O LORD, for I hide myself in you (Psalm 143:8-9).

The Second Day

I slept a few hours that Sunday night, then was awake for some time, and fell asleep close to 5:00 a.m.; I was awakened at 5:55 with a physical thump on my forehead! It felt exactly like the doctor testing one's reflexes with a decisive thump under the kneecap with a rubber mallet. This "wake-up call" had the same feeling and strength as that thump. I was amused, unhurt, and wondering what kind of angel is sent by God with a rubber mallet to wake up Jill. Whoever it was, I was now awake, and began to worship my Messiah.

From 6:00 until 8:15, I praised Him in a spontaneous way, speaking and singing at great length about the value of Yeshua's Blood, and recounting His acts toward our Fathers. I praised my way through the flood, the ark of safety, Abraham and his sacrifice of Isaac, Passover, and the blood of the Lamb.

At certain points, I would sing to the Lord a known song on the subject of my praise, such as "Lamb of God" by Twila Paris. I recounted the times of the Judges, Saul, David, Kings and the two exiles of Israel from the Land. I ended by declaring that in the "fullness of time," He came to dwell upon the face of the earth (Gal. 4:4).

At 8:15, I began my coffee talk with Yeshua in my special chair. To my joy and relief, my awareness of His presence had returned to me during my time of worship, and it did not depart again. I believe that the half a day, in which I couldn't feel Him with me, was a test of my faith and perseverance.

During coffee, I read aloud Psalms 2, 5 and 13. I then sang a heartbreaking song from Psalm 13 called "How Long O Lord" by Marty Goetz.[7] This transparent ballad evokes pain and longing for Him to reveal Himself, and always brings me to tears. In this psalm, David is pleading with the Lord to come and show Himself a faithful friend and defender, but he is also reminding his soul of the kindness God has shown him in the past. I wish that every believer could hear this remarkable song of lovesick yearning.

Afterwards, I knelt for my intercessory prayer time, and then, at around 10:30, I waited on Him, wearing the tallit. During this session, He spoke to me with more clarity than I have generally known. I could "see" Him with my spirit, and as He spoke, I could sometimes perceive even the expression on His face. This was remarkable to me, but I had to fight the urge to doubt the reality of what was happening. It was during this late morning session, that I received the following vision, which would shake my foundations and test the quality and reliability of my faith walk until the last day.

Martyrdom!

As I was waiting on Him, His Spirit told me to begin to cry, "Abba" (Daddy in Hebrew). I started to say it in a normal voice, but He urged me to groan and cry out, "Abba," with much longing and sadness in my voice. I obeyed this prompting, and began to cry out "Abba," and the emotion of deep sadness began to fill me, in keeping with the tone of my cry.

As I cried out, I suddenly saw myself on a terribly crowded city street, as a lost little girl; I was crying out for my Daddy, but could not find Him in the crowd. I was small and could not see over the heads of many people in front of me, but I knew He was somewhere ahead of me in the crowd. I kept crying, "Abba," hoping to catch up to Him or cause Him to turn around, but couldn't find Him.

I then knew that the crowded street was in a particular European country. I immediately looked to my left, to verify my location. I wanted to see which language was written over the shops. I saw two shops, and their names were written in that language. In between these two was a shop whose name designated death. A woman came out of that shop, and said to me, "As you can see, people are buying and selling, and going about their business, but people like you, we will chop off your heads." Then she began to pull me into her shop. Then I heard a voice say, *"Would you like that?"*

This was getting too strange for me, and I ignored that question, thinking it could not possibly be from the Lord. What kind of a question is that? I then heard the question again, but in my doubt and fear that I was entering a bizarre and imaginary world, I did not respond to the question again. At this point, I came out of the vision and back in my "waiting" mode in the rocking chair.

The Lord then seemed to change the subject abruptly and began to instruct me about matters concerning my brother. Neither of us mentioned the European scenario or the outrageous question someone had just posed to me. He then spoke to me about business, stock investments and certain medical provisions I was to purchase. He was brusque and business-like in His tone and expression. This conversation, along with His asking me to play a small game about trust from my childhood with Him, brought us to midday.

After lunch, I read for half an hour and the Lord then asked me to worship. I spent more than an hour singing, dancing and playing the guitar to Him. I then began to feel the urge for something dramatic to happen; my dear friends and intercessors were praying for my three days, and I was hoping to experience something worthy of three days of seclusion! I prayed for a manifestation of His presence, and then waited again in my rocking chair.

The Lord Jesus told me I was way too serious and asked me to play another game, in which I stood up and did some funny exercises. This was to loosen me up from the grip of my expectations which had formed into a demand that something happen. The game got me laughing, and I knew it was wrong to expect high drama.

We had a conversation about why I felt pressure to have an experience and what my friends might be expecting from my set-apart time. Finally, the Lord told me I did not owe anyone a dramatic story. He was just enjoying being with me and wanted me to feel the same. I told Him that at the beginning, I was just happy to be with Him 24/7, but then I fell into the trap of expectations, which can lead to disappointment, frustration, self-doubt, self-pity, or even anger.

Would You Like That?

Then Yeshua solemnly reminded me that the feelings of His presence will not always be there. He began to explain to me the morning's vision. He said, *"The reason I had you crying out 'Abba' like a lost child, is because this is exactly how you will feel at the end. You will cry out for Me but will not be able to find Me. You need to prepare to hang on. That is what the Scriptures mean by, "He who overcomes..."*

I started to cry at this unwelcome prediction. I said, "I don't want to feel like a lost child, calling out for You and not finding You."

The Lord calmly said, *"You will feel that way."*

I stifled my feeling of abandonment and asked Him about the vision. "What was that scene I saw? Were you actually showing me my future martyrdom in [that nation]?" I asked this, not believing it could possibly represent a real future event.

Immediately, I heard the familiar voice say, *"Would you like that?"*

I was confused again by this strange question and decided to ignore it once again. It was unanswerable. How could this be the voice of Yeshua? I looked away and was silent.

After a moment, I head the question yet again. *"Would you like that?"*

Finally, I thought I'd better answer, in case this was the real Yeshua asking me a question. I looked at Him and said, "How could anyone *like* martyrdom?" There was a bit of an edge in my voice.

He immediately said, *"But you know what is set before you. Would you like that?"*

I now knew this was the voice of my Lord. I looked away and thought for one or two minutes. I remembered the rewards for martyrdom in the Book of Revelation. I tried to picture the excellence of heaven waiting for me, although my mind could not imagine any glorious scene. I thought of a crown for those who finished the race and did not love their lives unto death. Was any other answer possible? I looked back at Him and said, "Yes, for what is set before me, I would like that." The Lord then continued His prediction on the feeling of abandonment. *"It will feel like I am not there, as I felt abandoned on the cross. I was not really abandoned by My Father, but it felt that way. You will feel that way too, but I will come when you need Me, and I will rescue you by death."*

Yeshua then looked at me with a very concerned expression, and added, *"It will not be an easy death."* Was this dialogue really happening? A staggering sense of unreality set in, and I was now very afraid. What did I just agree to? This last statement was not what I wanted to hear, and I began to wonder how difficult it might be. The part which troubled me the most were His statements about feeling abandoned.

The Lord had also prophesied to Peter about the death by which he would glorify God; perhaps this was not easy for Peter to contemplate either, as the Lord's words can sometimes be hard to bear.

"I tell you the truth, when you were younger you dressed yourself and went where you wanted; but when you are old you will stretch out your hands, and someone else will dress you and lead you where you do not want to go." Jesus said this to indicate the kind of death by which Peter would glorify God (John 21:18-19).

Peter immediately turned to look at John and asked the Lord, "What about him?" Peter wondered if John would also have to suffer, perhaps seeking comfort from this stark prediction of his future crucifixion. The Lord told him,

If I want him to remain alive until I return, what is that to you? You must follow me (John 21:22).

The Lord loves equally both those who are martyred and those who will remain alive until His return. We must know with assurance that whichever destiny He has purposed for us is the very best; we must never compare our destiny to anyone else. The Lord only does what is best for His children, although I did not fully grasp this at the time of this startling revelation during my three days. Our brother Peter's honest emotions and reactions are very comforting to me; it is so easy to relate to his weaknesses and mistakes, and yet the Lord loved Peter so much!

The Prison of Fear

I did not have time to process all these emotions. For some reason, the Lord ended this conversation by talking once more about my friends' expectations and what I would tell them when I was released. Because I was now feeling shock and fear about the future I had just embraced, as well as submerged anger about His statements that I would not be able to find Him, my tone of voice became overly casual and slightly disrespectful. I was making a poor attempt to cover up my overwhelming emotions, which were too fresh to tame or ignore. So I feigned indifference.

The moment I recognized the disrespect which had crept into my own voice, the Lord Jesus said, *"Will you kneel and worship Me?"*

I put my feelings aside and worshipped Him on my face; I acknowledged Him as my King, Savior and *Mashiach* (Messiah). I then took Communion with great reverence and love for His sacrifice.

That evening, I sang sweet worship to Him as the candles burned low. But when I turned out the lights and was alone with my thoughts, I began to suffer from mental terror, which would continue to oppress me for more than a month after this encounter. That very night, I began to allow my mind to imagine what they would do to me. The possibilities were vast, and Satan, with the help of my imagination, showed me a variety of hideous scenarios with increasing degrees of cruelty. For the third night in a row, I slept very little. However, unlike the first two nights, this night was replete with a new justification for my insomnia: Fear!

> *I tell you, my friends, do not be afraid of those who kill the body and after that can do no more. But I will show whom you should fear: Fear him who, after the killing of the body, has power to throw you into hell* (Luke 12:4-5).

The Third Day

Early in the morning, I worshiped the Lord in bed, playing my guitar again. It is important that we learn to worship Him without the benefit of CDs, which may not always be possible in the near future. I also sang for a while without accompaniment. Then we had our last coffee talk, or so I thought. During this peaceful conversation, the Lord Yeshua told me that over the past two days, I had offered Him many words, songs and acts of devotion. Today, apart from my regular prayers and waiting time, I was free to read and rest for the afternoon, until He would release me before sunset. I was very joyful to hear this; I was reading *Books of Destiny* by Paul Keith Davis[8], and was looking forward to a relaxing afternoon of reading.

We discussed Psalm 45 in detail during this talk. The Lord gave me much insight about the Bride and about Messiah's dynasty of spiritual sons and daughters spoken of in verse 16. Matthew shows us Yeshua's Hebraic genealogy, as He sprang from the line of His father, David, and the fathers before him. Though Yeshua had no physical offspring, He gave birth to many spiritual children whom the Father gave Him. As Psalm 45:16 states: "Your sons will take the place of your fathers; You will make the princes throughout the land."

The Lord showed me His end-time company of sons and daughters doing the works that Yeshua did on earth—a powerful army of healing evangelists, fiery worshipers and anointed prophets would fill the earth. The latter anointing on these radical sons and daughters would surpass the former anointing on the fathers, David, and the prophets of Israel.

> *And afterward, I will pour out my Spirit on all people. Your sons and daughters will prophesy, Your old men will dream dreams, your young men will see visions. Even on my servants, both men and women, I will pour out my Spirit in those days* (Joel 2:28-29).

God would no longer only pour out His spirit of prophecy on a few select men of Israel, a tiny handful among the multitudes of peoples on the earth. In these days, He would pour His Spirit out on all flesh: young and old, Jew and Gentile, male and female, rich and poor! All who loved Him would do exploits at this time and would carry a greater anointing than 'the fathers' whom we greatly honor and love. I felt great excitement as the Lord showed me these things from this amazing wedding Psalm.

This conversation was the most intimate time of sharing we had enjoyed since the three days began. He also told me, *"During your free time this after-noon, you may not think about torture or martyrdom. I will be with you then, and it will be over, but we have so much work to do before that happens!"* I knew that the Lord was excited, and He wanted me to be joyful and excited about all the work we will do together, and not to dwell on the dark hour that will come. My spirit wanted to obey Him in this matter, but my mind would prove to be a raging battlefield, in which I did not achieve any victory or obedience to this admonition for quite a long time.

> *For you did not receive a spirit that makes you a slave again to fear, but you re-ceived a spirit of sonship. And by him we cry "Abba, Father!"* (Rom. 8:15)

His Respect Towards Us!

During my prayer time, the Lord began to teach me more about His char-acter, as He reviewed with me conversations we had shared over the last three days. I was newly struck by His attributes of gentleness, kindness, humility and respect for us! I realized that during the three days, and in fact, throughout all of my believing life, He rarely commanded me to do something. Very often, it would have been easier for me to receive a direct command from Him than to agonize over the many difficult decisions I had made over the years. But so often, His response was, "What would you prefer? How is your heart leading you? Would you like that?" Of course, this last question had taken on new sig-nificance forever!

I remembered that the Lord has often given me choices. Sometimes, He would indicate a spiritual advantage to one path, but other times, I had no idea which would be better. Despite my pleading for answers in the past, the King of kings and Lord of lords rarely dictated what I should do. It surprised me to fi-nally learn that He had deliberately not told me what to do, out of respect for my choices; I had previously assumed that I wasn't close enough to Him to hear His answers. This put all of my history with Him in a new light.

The Lord has every right to dictate; after all, He is the King of the universe, why shouldn't He give commands? We know from Scripture that He does, in fact, give commands, and I have certainly received commands from time to time as well. However, Yeshua's humble heart and gentle character cause Him to respect the choices of His people, and all people, for that matter. Even when we do not choose the best way, the Lord will rarely violate our God-given free will. The Lord conveyed to me in deep and permanent way during this prayer session that all obedience must be totally voluntary.

I am aware that Scripture, as translated in the KJV reads, "God is not a respecter of persons," and that some might object to my contention that He respects our free will. However, a careful reading of Acts 10:34, and Deuteronomy 10:17 from which Peter is quoting, says that God does not show favoritism or partiality, but judges all men with equity and righteousness. These verses are not in any way contradictory to what He showed me about His humility and respect for our decisions, even when they are not the best decisions.

The Lord Jesus also taught me about the "Freewill Offering" as it applies to financial contributions, apart from the regular tithe. Again, I had often asked Him to just tell me to whom to give, and how much. He explained that the decision was truly mine, which is why it is called a "freewill offering." It tests and proves what is in my heart to do voluntarily and is not forced upon me by a command.

After this prayer time, I waited on the Lord, and this session was filled with much music (in my spirit) and a vision of Yeshua dancing joyfully with His children, wearing the tallit, in a Hebraic circle dance at a Messianic congregation. I heard many songs in my spirit, to accompany much dancing with my brothers and sisters, and also with the Lord.

Physically, I remained in my rocking chair, but my spirit danced up a storm. When I say "my spirit danced," let it be clear that I was not having an "out of body experience." I merely mean that I could see my spirit dancing with the Lord; this version of me was dressed beautifully, and looked younger, radiant and energized, beyond my natural earthly appearance and energy level. It is like the "real me" is trying to get out of the limitations of my frail frame and burst forth in heavenly joy and celebration.

A Plea for Confirmation

After lunch, I was planning to read my book. I did try to read for a little while, but something was deeply troubling me under the surface of my relaxing afternoon. I was seriously doubting the objective reality of the vision and conversation the Lord and I had exchanged, concerning my martyrdom in another country, a country to which I had never felt called.

I was very aware that before the sun would set on this, the third day, our in-

tense and intimate time would be over. Did I really have enough concrete revelation on which to base my understanding of my own destiny and death? This
would surely affect my family! There was a part of me that hoped I hadn't heard
it at all; I wondered if I had imagined the whole scenario, but I didn't want the
Lord to be angry with me for doubting. There was a part of me that hoped I
had heard it because that would mean He was really with me in my room, revealing important information to me about the future.

As I attempted to read, I wrestled with these thoughts, while battling mental
images of a violent and prolonged death. I could not afford to let the sun go
down on my three days, without settling this critical matter in my mind. I *had*
to talk to Him one more time! But would He be angry with me for doubting?
Should I hide my doubts from Him and just accept what I had already received?
Did He not already know my thoughts and doubts? Would it not be better to
tell Him what He already knows?

I got in my rocking chair again and looked directly at the One I could not
see. I told Him, "Please, let my Lord not be angry with me, but these conversations with You and the vision, only seemed to be in my mind. You know that I
really do have some measure of faith. You know that I read Choo's book,[9] and I
believed every word of it. Choo saw You with her eyes, and You took her out of
her body to heaven. I only hear You in my mind, without visual or audible manifestation. Even a manifestation of Your glory has been lacking. How can I know
for sure that the real You was telling me about my death? This is a most serious
matter. If I have found favor with my Lord, please give me some confirmation,
anything You would like, to show me that this really happened, and is really the
truth."

My final plea was ended. I closed my eyes and waited, and the Holy Spirit
said, *"Pray in tongues for a while."* I began to pray in tongues, which seemed particularly fluid and articulate at this moment. I continued for about fifteen minutes, and then the heavy presence of the Lord began to descend on me. His
presence increased until I was overshadowed by His glory, to the point that I
could neither speak nor move. It remained like this for a significant period of
time.

He said, *"Is this confirmation enough for you?"*
I said "yes" in my thoughts, because I could not speak.
He said, forcefully, *"Who is standing before you?"*
I weakly said in my heart, "The King of Glory" and tried to move my lips.
He said again, *"Who is standing before you?"*
I said, "The King of Glory." Then I meekly added, "So I'll be martyred in
[the nation]?"
He said, *"Yes, you'll be martyred in [the nation]. Now stop doubting."*

Released

It was now about 4:30 p.m. I had received sufficient confirmation that this revelation was true and really from my Lord. My strength was gone, and He told me to rest and recover in bed for half an hour. After exactly half an hour, my strength came back to me.

Then I took Communion with the Lord for the third time in three days. When I finished Communion, I remained on my knees, and asked the Lord if He would release me from my time of seclusion. I then saw Him, with the eyes of my spirit, standing in front of where I was kneeling. I watched Him blow the Shofar (the ram's horn) over me. He blew two sharp tones that I recognized, and He blessed me in Hebrew. He pronounced the priestly blessing over the Israelites found in Numbers 6:22-27, but modified it with feminine endings for my sake.

He then spoke a brief personal blessing in conversational Hebrew. He told me that these days had been very pleasant, to which I replied, *"Gam li"* ("For me, also.") He also used a phrase that I thought meant "a much loved daughter" but weeks later, after looking in a book of Hebrew verb constructions[10], it seems the Lord said, "you are My daughter, very much in love." He told me I was blessed and released at this time. I fell at His feet and thanked Him and worshipped Him. It was 6:00 p.m., one hour before sunset. I got up, showered, and returned to my waiting family and immediately immersed myself in my normal responsibilities.

The Day After

The next morning, I was back in my normal routine, which included worship and prayer. I began to thank the Lord with great intensity for these awesome three days with Him. I felt very happy and "in love with Him." Interestingly, I had not yet checked the form of that Hebrew verb, and yet immediately after the three days, I experienced being "in love" with Him for the first time. If indeed that is the blessing with which He blessed me, it was effectual even though I misunderstood His meaning.

I started to recount to the Lord the events of the day before, concerning my doubts about the martyrdom vision. As I retold the experience of His glory overshadowing me, and while I was still describing it to Him, His Presence came upon me very strongly again, and remained for a long time.

While I was in the glory, I saw Him fairly clearly with my eyes closed, as He stood over me. I was not writing as He spoke, but afterwards, recorded my best recollection of His words to me: *"I now know that you love Me with all your heart. You have shown Me your heart, and have not withheld from Me anything that was in your heart. Even though I know the thoughts of people's hearts, if they don't share them with Me, I don't really know them* (He is referring to knowing the person, not the thoughts) *because I will not violate their privacy. This is part of My humble and respectful character which I was showing you yesterday.*

"*You have proven that you will just enjoy being with Me, even if I don't manifest in any dramatic way you would have liked. You are truly My friend. Now I can trust you, because you proved you will be My friend and enjoy My company, without expecting anything from Me.*"

The Lord then granted me the following experience, which was a spiritual event, seen by the eyes of my spirit. The Lord took two of His fingers from His right hand and dipped them into the wound in His left hand, and His fingers had blood on them. He put this blood on my forehead (it was not physical blood), and He said, "*You are sealed forever. You are one of My own ones, and you will be with Me forever.*"

I know that all true believers in the Lord Jesus are bought with His blood and sealed by His Spirit (2 Cor. 1:22; Eph. 1:13). The Lord did not explain to me the meaning of this sealing, and I will not speculate as to its exact significance.

After He did this astonishing thing, I knew I would not deny Him during a painful death, because He said I would be with Him forever. In the past, I was always afraid that under physical duress, I would deny Him to stop the pain. I know now that He will keep all who love Him safely in His hand until the last day. I praise His most holy name!

Transparency of Heart

This last word which Yeshua spoke to me in the holy moment of sealing me is one of the most critical lessons that must be released from this book. It is extremely significant to notice that in giving me the most treasured seal of His own blood, the Lord did *not* commend me for volunteering to give my life for Him. He did not say, "Because you have offered to die for My name, I am sealing you forever." To me, this offer of martyrdom would seem the most sacrificial thing I could ever offer Him, and thus, the most worthy of reward.

Despite what I might have thought, this was not what He valued the most. The Lord Jesus valued most the fact that I withheld nothing from Him that was in my heart! He emphasized that many of His people keep things in their hearts, without telling Him. Many Christians may think, "He already knows all my thoughts. Why would I need to tell Him?" This is a natural question, but I cannot emphasize strongly enough that He wants, needs and requires His people to tell Him everything, regardless of the fact that He can read the thoughts of our heart.

This is so important to the Lord, that if we do not tell Him everything in our hearts, He warns, *"I don't really know them."* Yeshua was not saying that He doesn't know our thoughts unless we tell Him. He was saying that He never comes to fully *know* us as intimate friends, if we do not tell Him everything. In Hebrew, the verb "to know" is a most intimate word. It is not a passing acquaintance. When Adam became intimate with his wife, Eve, it says, "And Adam knew his wife." This is the way the Lord was using this word when He said, "if they don't tell Me, I never really know them." I was immediately reminded of the chilling verses in Matthew 7:21-23, where "believers" come to Him, reminding Him of the great works they did in His name; but He says, "I never *knew* you. Away from Me, you lawless ones!"

Since He calls them "lawless ones," there may have been hidden sins in the lives of these disobedient Christians. However, the Lord is also claiming to have never known them; it is too horrible to imagine hearing these words from Him. I need to encourage every reader to be utterly transparent with the Lord; never assume that because He knows your thoughts, you do not need to verbalize them. This warning is one of His strongest motivations for the writing of this book. It has changed my life as well.

Additional Confirmation

Due to the unparalleled seriousness of the revelation about my martyrdom, and in addition to the awesome glory which the Lord revealed to me to confirm it, I knew it would be right to submit this testimony to an objective pastoral and prophetic authority. I did not want to testify about what He had shown me without some external confirmation.

Obviously, I shared this with my own family. Then I shared this testimony, as outlined in this chapter, with my pastors, John and Sandra Shantz of Spring City Fellowship in Spring City, Pennsylvania. They are a godly and upright pastoral couple, with a long and generous history of ministry; I respect their years of service to the Body of Messiah, their witness of the Lord Jesus, and their integrity.

I sat in their office and explained the entire account of my three days to them, and emphasized the details of the martyrdom portion. Pastor John and Sandy were prayerful and gracious to support and confirm my belief that it was indeed the Lord Yeshua who spoke this to me, and that I was not deceived about this matter. I am so grateful to this generous couple for prayerfully supporting me in many areas of my journey, ministry and personal life. As this book is completed, they will be among the first to read it, and I bless them from my heart.

In addition, I sent this testimony to two highly prophetic individuals, whose ministries are not connected to my church, to me personally, or to each other's ministry. These people are widely respected for their integrity, character and prophetic trustworthiness. It was humbling for me to receive independent confirmations from each of them, according to their individual styles of expression and communication with the Lord Yeshua. After this gift from the Lord, I have not questioned the reliability of this revelation, and feel comfortable testifying of it publicly.

CHAPTER 7

LOVESICK AND TERRIFIED

After the three days, I began to feel overwhelmed with lovesick sadness for the Lord's presence. I missed Him continually, no matter how much I tried to carve out time for worship and prayer. I cried several times a day but could never explain what was making me sad. The intensity of the three days had placed a demand for Him in my soul, and His final blessing had identified me as "very much in love."

One morning, Katya and I were on a ministry trip and were having breakfast in a rustic mountain café. We were having a pleasant conversation, when the waitress brought our food. I took a sip of my coffee and burst into tears. Katya asked me what was wrong, and all I could say was, "I miss Him." Obviously, the coffee triggered strong and intimate memories that were now only reminders of what I was lacking.

During that early phase, I was talking to the Lord about what a sharp acceleration was occurring in my relationship with Him. It seemed to be increasing exponentially, compared to the last 30 years. He said, *"Yes, I have advanced you quickly to a new level of intimacy with Me."*

I asked the Lord, with tears, why I felt so lost and disoriented, happy, yet sad and confused. He answered me: *"When My people reach this level of intimacy with Me, they begin to feel an acute longing for heaven. The things and pleasures of this life no longer give them any pleasure. The world begins to feel like a hostile, inhospitable and uninhabitable wasteland. The sights and sounds of this earth are disturbing to them, and they feel like strangers in a strange land, wanderers. They feel forlorn and lost, and painfully aware that this earth is not their home. This is how you feel and will continue to feel until I take you home to be with Me forever, the Blessed Hope."*

This condition that the Lord so beautifully described has remained with me to this day. It has not faded, as the memory of my three days faded into everyday life. This pain is part of the price we must pay for intimacy with Him. Our fathers David, Solomon and Paul felt this pain in their hearts, and the Lord Yeshua was "consumed with zeal for His Father's House" (John 2:17).

All night long on my bed I looked for the one my heart loves; I looked for him but did not find him (Song of Songs 3:1).

As the deer pants for streams of water, so my soul pants for you, O God. My soul thirsts for God, for the living God. When can I go and meet with God? My tears have been my food, day and night, while men say to me all day long, "Where is your God?" (Psalm 42:1-3)

Not only so, but we ourselves, who have the firstfruits of the Spirit, groan inwardly as we wait eagerly for our adoption as sons, the redemption of our bodies (Romans 8:23).

The Reign of Terror

During the same period of weeks that I was suffering the constant ache in my heart for the Lord, I was also suffering severe mental torment over the martyrdom scenarios that were playing out on the stage of my mind, many times each day and night. As weeks passed, I realized I could not stop these scenes from coming, and only sometimes could I cut them short. My mind seemed to need to play the scene out to the bitter end. Or was Satan tormenting me, to cause me to mistrust the goodness of God?

It was almost like being in hell. I rebuked these thoughts and repeatedly asked the Lord to take them away. I gave the burden to Him and struggled to abort the scenarios before they carried me away. They just kept coming and coming, and I started to become depressed, crying at random moments during the day. My family did not know what was wrong, and I was too ashamed of my cowardice to speak about it. I was subliminally angry at the Lord for revealing something to me that I obviously couldn't handle.

It didn't feel like an honor, although I knew what the Bible taught. I had been teaching in the churches for many years that we will not be exempt from Jesus' warnings to His disciples that we will be hated and killed for His name. But teaching about it in a theoretical way is completely different from coming face to face with the absolute certainty of a painful martyrdom. When it is just a good teaching, one can still say, "But the Lord knows I am not brave, and require prayer before going to the dentist. I am not a good candidate for this." Surely, He will choose courageous characters, like "Braveheart" and the apostle Paul for such an honor. Why would He choose a jellyfish who faints at the sight of blood and cannot endure any pain with courage, stoic silence, or acceptance?

Along with my great fear, came overwhelming shame at my cowardice. For a week or two, I kept it to myself, and did not even tell my closest friends how afraid I was. This led to depression; I made a desperate attempt to act normal, when I was falling apart.

One night, my close friend Dave called me, and I confessed the depth of my fear to him. I told him, "Out of the three most wonderful days of my life, came the most terrible certainty that I would be given into the hands of cruel and merciless men. Before these three days, I could always 'hope for the best' about an easy death, but now I know for certain that I will feel abandoned, and it will not be easy."

Dave gave me excellent counsel, reminding me that our loving Father would only have revealed this to me if it were for my good. He also emphasized that I would not be abandoned by the Lord, although it would feel that way. He helped me to understand that I would be able to help others in the future, who would be very afraid of their martyrdom, as I had been. He also prayed for me as he has done in previous times of crisis and fear in my life, and ministered to me in comforting prayer over the phone. Who can put a value on a friend like this?

On another occasion during the same period of time, Katya came to my house, having received a word that the Father wanted to comfort me, but not knowing anything was wrong because I had kept my terror and shame very private. As soon as she told me this word, I was finally honest with her and with the Lord, and allowed myself to mourn my own death, and the shortness of time.

This transparency allowed me to weep with my precious sister, and to be held in the Father's arms. He lovingly said to me, *"I'm totally on your side."* I felt his strong presence, as did Katya. The reservoir of pain, fear and shame was released in His tender embrace, and I was comforted. We serve a God of comfort and compassion, a great High Priest who is able to sympathize with our weaknesses.

Since those awful weeks, the Lord has given me much comfort and biblical strategies which free His people from fear; it is never His will for us to suffer fear of the future. The Lord Yeshua also showed me how He approached His own cruel death.

Even on His last night on earth, when He knew exactly what would occur within a few hours, He was eagerly desiring the Passover meal with His disciples, and was teaching them up until the last moment. Our Messiah was not so sick with fear that He could not enjoy this meal and celebration with His *y'didim* (beloved friends). The Lord Jesus was joyful and loving, always thinking of imparting to them, and not dwelling on His own impending torture and terrible execution. If He could behave this way, only hours before His suffering, how much more should I behave as He did, when the interval to my departure is still a matter of years, rather than hours?

The Lord has given me some additional revelation in order to comfort me and reduce my fear of this event, although He has not minimized its difficulty. It is important for me to share His goodness and faithfulness, and to testify that all of His plans are truly the best for our lives. He will never leave or forsake His own ones, for "precious in the sight of the Lord is the death of His saints" (Psalm 116:15).

The Lord was preparing me for this destiny over the years, but I did not grasp it. Seven months before my three days, He gave me a word which at the time, seemed too terrible to write down in my journal. I had just taken Communion with Him in my room, and I thanked Him for His sacrifice. This word came into my mind at that moment, and I wrote it down, despite my reluctance to commit to writing what I was hearing: *"You have been sanctified by My Blood and My Body. I was torn asunder for your sake, and you will be torn asunder for My sake. Do not fear, for I AM with you to cover you and shield you from harm. I AM your Savior, the one who saves you, so when ferocious beasts come to devour you, put your trust in Me, for they will come. Do not be surprised when they are released to attack and devour you, for I have told you ahead of time. My strength will comfort and sustain you, and you will not be harmed if you trust in Me.*

"No one will help you, do not look for it, for it shall be terrible for you; but I AM with you and I will not forsake you when they come to devour you. I will not give you over to them, but they will seek to terrify you and you must not let fear devour you. I AM your protection and true shelter from the storm. My enemies who hate Me will hate My people. You are one with Me, and that will include being hated with Me. So put your trust in Me, little one, and you will be safe. Hide in Me, for I AM your true shelter."

I hoped this word might be metaphorical, rather than literal. I tried to imagine my enemies punishing me with financial or legal action. My mind wanted to deny what this stark prediction seemed to be saying. It also seemed contradictory that I would be "devoured," and yet He "would not give me over." Likewise, how could I be "torn asunder" and yet "not be harmed?" It did not make sense, and yet I remembered that in Luke 21:16-19, He said, "they will put some of you to death. All men will hate you because of Me. But not a hair of your head will perish. By standing firm you will gain life." Somehow, we will be killed and yet be kept safe and alive. That could also sound contradictory, if not for our understanding of the martyr's grace (Acts 7:59) and the resurrection of the body (1 Cor. 15:42, 52-55).

One other word of great encouragement He gave me during those frightening weeks following the three days was this: *"I have called you, and have seen your tears and cries before Me. I AM not unkind or callous to offer you the destiny I have offered you. I do all things out of kindness, and out of the goodness of My heart. You are special, honored and favored by Me. This is why I have shown you how you will glorify Me in your death, even as Peter glorified Me in his death, though he did not wish to go there, nor does any man, nor did I.*

"But My Father's perfect will is higher than the will of His children, and those who willingly suffer for His name's sake will reign with Him forever, even seated on His throne with Him. Those who suffer unwillingly, as many will in these last days, will only receive the rewards of what they have done on this earth. It is an honor to volunteer, and you will not regret that decision, though it will not be an easy path. Those who seek to save their life will lose it and those who voluntarily lose it for My sake will find it again, whole and perfectly restored.

"Even the hairs on your head are precious to Me. I will not allow you to suffer beyond your ability to endure. Trust Me to take you home at the right and perfect moment. The Father's plan and will must be permitted by those who love Him and love Me. He requires voluntary obedience, as you spoke about in church yesterday.

"Be of good cheer. I have saved you forever, and I will rescue you from the paw of the lion and the teeth of the bear. Stand firm and secure, and you will see My salvation. Hide yourself in Me. Hide in Me. Learn to abide in the Secret Place of the Most High, and even the most terrible will be bearable when covered in My Grace and Abiding Presence. You are safe, so rejoice in Me, and do all the work I have prepared for you, and you will receive a crown of life that will never perish. Thus says your Elohim. Yeshua HaMashiach has come in the flesh. And He loves you, Jill. Amen v'amen."

Come, Lord Yeshua.

CHAPTER 8

"COFFEE TALKS"

During the three days, I noticed that out of all the varied spiritual disciplines I practiced, the sweetest and most intimate moments were our coffee
talks. I did not think this had much to do with the actual coffee, although it is a
fine beverage that I have loved since childhood. However, something about our
interaction during coffee talk was quite different than the other vital disciplines
of prayer, waiting, worship, or reading Scripture. Perhaps the best description is
"intimate friendship." I have thought about this quite a bit, since the term
"coffee talk" is not found in the common Christian vocabulary, nor is intimate
friendship spoken of in most church services.

In John 15, Yeshua says, "Greater love has no one than this, that he lay down
his life for his friends." The modern Hebrew translation of the New Testament
uses the word *y'did* for friend, rather than the more common word, *chaver*.
Y'did is the same root as "David" which means "dearly beloved," rather than the
simple word for friend. He is calling us not mere acquaintances, but uses the
strongest word for beloved, intimate friends. Jonathan and David were *y'didim*:
beloved, covenant friends. We will look more deeply at the covenant friendship
between two people in the next chapter. But at this moment, we explore the intimacy between Yeshua and His own ones.

Make an Appointment

Most believers know that God is omnipresent. He is truly everywhere at one
time. He can visit one thousand churches on the same morning. He can answer
the specific questions and prayers of ten thousand of His children at the same
moment, in different parts of the globe. He can be personally present at the
birth and martyrdom of hundreds of His own ones in a split second. His Holy
Spirit lives inside each individual who has accepted Yeshua's infinitely costly
sacrifice, the only way to be restored to a loving relationship with the Holy One
of Israel. He knows the stars by name and could easily create geological upheaval by slightly touching the rotation of the earth. So what in the world is a
coffee talk with Yeshua? Is He truly making a personal appointment with one
ordinary believer and sitting down to have a conversation over a cup of coffee?

Yes, apparently He is doing exactly that, for this is what I have discovered, and this was His motivation for the writing of this book. He wants this intimate relationship with each one of His children, those who yearn for Him as for a most cherished friend. The Lord wants to know us fully and to hear us transparently bare our hearts to Him, as if we were telling our most trusted friend our secrets. It really doesn't matter if one enjoys drinking coffee, tea or cocoa. The time it takes to sip a steaming beverage only represents a leisurely, lingering interval of fellowship and relaxed conversation; no one is looking at the clock, and no one is racing off to do something more important than converse. Apparently, He has all the time in the world! Do we?

When I received the word recorded in Chapter 5 about what He desired of me, I noticed that He requested a "coffee talk." However, I didn't realize at that time that He literally wanted me to sit down with Him as I sat down with Ariela every morning for coffee and conversation. After I received this word, a schedule adjustment permitted me to have coffee with both Keren and Ari most mornings. That portion of the word was as follows:

> In the same way that you have your coffee time with your daughter, I just want a coffee time with My daughter, to laugh, cry, talk or just sit together. It is *so* precious to Me. Is it precious to you? I know it is. Just come. Sometimes there is much you and your daughter share, other times it's a little more quiet, but your time together is treasured. Come to Me with the treasures of your heart, mind and soul…I am waiting for you.

During the three days, I sat and had my coffee with the Lord, as I would normally have it with the girls. When the three days were ended, I didn't think about continuing this version of fellowship between us. About three weeks later, I heard His Spirit say, *"Could we have a coffee talk once a week?"*

I was very happy to comply with this request. For several months, we met once a week, always on a Wednesday morning. Keren and Ariela knew this was my morning with Him, and I had coffee with them on the other six days of the week.

After a while, the Lord requested that we meet three times a week. I was partly excited and partly nervous about this request. It was a big adjustment for me, and by my negative reaction, He showed me a weakness in my heart.

"Why was it so hard for you when I increased the frequency of our coffee talks? Did it expose a weakness in your trust or character? Did you want more of Me or less of Me?"

This question convicted me, but I didn't yet understand why I was so reluctant to meet more often. At first, this was the answer I gave Him:

"When we were having a 'date day' once a week it seemed special and exciting. I went away full and satisfied. I was afraid that three times a week would feel routine and common, and neither of us would have much to say." This reason was true to some extent, but was not my real problem. However, the Lord addressed my "excuse."

"Don't you think I have a lot more to teach you and say to you?"

"Yes."

"What if I wanted to talk to you every day, would that be a problem?"

"No."

I then realized what the real problem was. To explain the problem, I need to describe the true spiritual atmosphere of a coffee talk. To hear the phrase, it sounds like a very relaxed, casual interlude, where I sit back, sip coffee, and Jesus and I have a comfortable chat, like "old friends on the porch in summer."

While it may sound like this, it is, in fact, nothing like this! It is quite different from what the name implies. It sounds easy and fun, but it is neither of these. It is enriching, rewarding, tiring, thrilling, exhilarating, humbling and unsettling at the same time.

Our Lord Yeshua, first of all, is a vast and complex Person; He is unpredictable, uncontainable and uncontrollable. His wisdom penetrates every crevice between soul and spirit (Hebrews 4:12-13), and His insight into our hearts is breathtaking. There is no possibility of a person feeling completely comfortable or relaxed with the Lord Jesus. This is not because He is unkind or intimidating. He is gentle, nurturing and understands our weakness. It is just because of who He is and who we are.

It is impossible for me to act "normal" when I am around Him; I feel small, immature and undone in a different way at every single coffee talk, no matter how many we might have in this life. However, I must add that I also feel loved, cherished, comforted, taught by the Best, honored, favored and abundantly blessed! But the difficulties outlined above explain the real reason for my reluctance to increase the frequency of our meetings to three times a week.

When I was meeting with Him once a week, I would approach each appointment in a nervous state. After my early morning worship, I would pace the room as the water boiled for my coffee. The reader may recall my description of a sheltered bride approaching an unknown wedding night, when I described my emotions leading up to the three days. Approaching each coffee talk carried the same type of anticipation, mingled with some nervous energy.

When I would finally sit down on the rocking chair and face Him, I would often shake and cry for the first five or ten minutes. I felt awkward about who would talk, and how I was to conduct myself. Occasionally, I would even doubt that we were having a "real" conversation. I felt concerned that my behavior, words or appearance would displease Him in some way, although He has never been anything but gracious and accepting of me, and has shown me unfailing love at every encounter.

Some talks seem more concrete than others, and it takes significant energy and concentration to participate with the Lord in these conversations, while stopping to journal the entire dialogue at various points during the talks. I realized that meeting three times a week would cause me to put a great deal of pressure on myself, and I was working way too hard at these encounters. Could I handle this three times a week, and did He mean for it to be this exhausting? Of course He did not.

By this increased request, the Lord was showing me that it was never His intention for me to add my own fear and nervous energy to these conversations, which He wished to be joyful and intimate. He wanted me to be more relaxed and happy with Him, without compromising my respect and reverence for Him.

Yeshua needed me to trust in His goodness and kindness toward me, and to believe that He and I were having a conversation which was delightful to both of us. It was my own sinful nature that added the extra pressure and exertion; His yoke is easy and His burden is light. I couldn't keep up the pressure of my former behavior, and this request for more appointments forced me to move into a more trusting and peaceful faith walk through the vehicle of coffee talks.

The Teacher's Lessons

The following testimonies are taken from actual coffee talks, as recorded in my journal. The Lord has shown me that much of the instruction He brings me during these talks would benefit all of His Bride and are not limited to me. In some cases, my dialogues with the Lord Jesus contain confidential material, as do every believer's intimate conversations with Him, but this is the exception rather than the norm.

These lessons primarily appear in the chronological order in which I received them. Most of them occurred after my three days in April 2006.

Because the material is taken from my journal in chronological order, the lessons may not flow together as a seamless narrative, as did the earlier chapters of my historical testimony. These words were given to me in this order by His sovereign plan, but whether or not they connect to each other in an obvious way is unclear to me. I pray they can be a blessing, even as separate nuggets of wisdom which are self-contained.

As with all extra-biblical prophetic words, I fully understand that the accuracy and reliability of these words are not to be compared with the trustworthiness and authority of the Scriptures, which are my sole basis for objective truth. Every revelation must be measured against God's Word, and if unbiblical content is discovered, (not to be confused with extra-biblical content) it must be discarded. I submit these words to the reader as I received them, to the best of my ability to hear and discern.

The Destruction of Yeshua's Body

One morning, before waiting on the Lord, I felt led to prepare Communion ahead of time, and bring it up to the room. While waiting, I was in His very strong presence. During this time, I felt He wanted me to take Communion, while still in the glory. This turned into the most unusual and painful Communion I have ever experienced. I was mostly incapacitated in His Presence, and my arm felt heavy as I forced myself to reach for the Matzoh cracker. With great effort, I retrieved the cracker.

As I began to bring it close to my mouth, I found myself deeply grieved, and I whimpered with reluctance to eat it. As I put it near my mouth, I sobbed piteously. I couldn't bear to eat it, but I kept trying to open my mouth, which was painful, tearful and almost impossible. I put the first bite in my mouth and tried to bite down. My jaw wasn't strong enough to break the cracker! I tried, and on the third attempt with great force, I felt the Matzoh break under my teeth. I sobbed and whimpered the whole time, sensing the crunching of human tissue; I perceived the tremendous force needed to crush and break the human body.

I was thinking of Yeshua's broken body, and it was awful. Each bite I took produced the same results. My heart was pleading with Him not to make me take another bite. By the third bite, I just wanted to put the last piece all in my mouth be done with it, but He wanted me to take one more bite. Finally, I ate the last piece, crushing it all with my teeth and feeling that I was breaking His body over and over with my cruel jaw mechanism. I saw my attackers cutting through my body before killing me, but felt no fear, because in the glory, it is impossible to feel fear.

The pain of what I was doing to Him was unbearable. I said, "I have eaten all of the Passover Lamb. None is left over. I have partaken of all of You" (Ex. 13:8-10).

Then I had to drink a full cup of His blood. How terrible it was, and I drank all of it, not leaving one drop. When I finished partaking fully in the Lord's suffering, He looked at me with a serious, searching and troubled look, as if He was trying to see if I "got it."

Then He said, *"Now do you understand what I have done for you?"*

I couldn't speak, but answered, "Yes, although I will never fully understand. But now I do understand what force it took to destroy Your body, and how I must partake of all Your flesh and all Your blood, or I will not know the fellowship of Your suffering" (Phil. 3:10; Rom. 8:17).

A Mother's Love

As the Lord and I were conversing, He redirected the subject by saying, *"Your mother never held you. You have a big hole in your heart. Let me comfort you."*

I was very surprised to hear this. My mother was a very industrious "Jewish mother," and I remembered the many things she did for us, but it was true: I could not remember her ever holding me. I knew she must have held me to put a bottle in my mouth, but I sensed the Lord was referring to the early childhood years, rather than the newborn stage.

There is a Psalm I often sing, written originally in Hebrew, and in fact, I had sung it to Him that very morning. It is Psalm 131:

> *My heart is not proud, O LORD, my eyes are not haughty; I do not concern myself with great matters or things too wonderful for me. But I have stilled and quieted my soul; like a weaned child with its mother, like a weaned child is my soul within me* (Psalm 131:1-2).

I usually cry when singing this Psalm, because of the tenderness of seeing myself as a safe and loved little toddler, leaning against her mother. Of course, "real life" does not feel like this safe place.

The Lord Jesus wanted to hold me, and love me with the tender and nurturing love of a mother. Despite the fact that He was a man, He has maternal attributes as well as the fatherly traits. We see this in Matthew 23:37. Because I did not want to feel the pain of what the Lord was revealing to me, I was reluctant for a while to allow Him to "hold me." Finally, I did let Him hold me like a mother, and I wept in His arms for a long time. This would not be the last time that I would need a mother's love, which I could only receive from Him.

There are so many aspects of the Lord's kind and gentle character, that we must not limit Him by gender. He is far greater than we can perceive and created us both, male and female, in His image (Gen 1:27).

> *Can a mother forget the baby at her breast and have no compassion on the child she has borne? Though she may forget, I will not forget you! See, I have engraved you on the palms of my hands; your walls are ever before me* (Isa. 49:15-16).

Submitting to His Will

We were discussing the Lord's omnipresence throughout my life. I was confessing that He was with me on the day of my birth and will be with me on the day of my death, to carry me out of this world as He carried me in. I was marveling that all of my days were written in His Book, before even one of them had occurred (Psalm 139:16).

Abruptly, the Lord Yeshua asked me a surprising question: *"Are you still mad at Me?"* He was referring to my lingering resentment about the strange way He had revealed my martyrdom to me, and His unsettling prediction about my being unable to find Him at the end, to the point of feeling abandoned. I answered Him, hoping that my reply was perfectly honest: "No, I'm not. Your will is perfect."

The Lord continued, *"You must fully embrace and agree with My plans for you. You can't kick against it, or squirm out of it, or wish it wouldn't happen. You are nailed with Me. You do not do your own will."* He reminded me of the verse: "For your sake we face death all day long; we are considered as sheep to be slaughtered" (Psalm 44:22; Rom. 8:36).

The Lord Jesus added, *"Do you fully agree to this martyrdom?"*

I sensed that if I would not completely agree to it at this moment, the opportunity would be permanently removed, although He did not actually say this. After all, I had been privately grieving and even regretting this difficult destiny. I could no longer afford to be double-minded, after all of His kindness and comfort to me.

I answered, "Yes." It was finished, and the time for resentment and second-guessing His plan was over.

The Lord then offered to tell me how I would die, in order to remove all the other potential scenarios from my thoughts. I told Him I was afraid to know, but He chose to tell me anyway, stating that knowing the truth is better than imagining numerous hideous possibilities. His motivation was to comfort me, without minimizing the difficulty of this event.

Yeshua then told me to promise Him that whenever this final scene would pop into my mind, I must give it to Him immediately and completely. I was reluctant to promise Him anything of the sort, knowing my proclivity to worry the matter into the ground. He continued to insist that I promise Him, and although I delayed for a while, He would not take "no" for an answer. I finally gave Yeshua my promise and have done my best to keep it until this day, although I cannot say I have always been quick enough to give it to Him.

The Lord then shared some confidential revelation concerning my family's future; I saw the loving and generous motives of His noble heart. I marveled at Yeshua's love; how could I have thought this compassionate Savior unkind?

Then Yeshua continued, *"Now I will tell you what I'm about to do to you now."* The Lord explained to me that He would pour out on me an anointing of power, which the Scriptures call "being clothed with power from on high" (Luke 24:49). I was shown the particular gifts of His Holy Spirit which I would receive.

The Lord then said, *"Would you like that?"* I burst out laughing, that He would use the exact phrase that He had used during the vision of the lost little girl on a foreign city street, and the subsequent martyrdom. That question, which had caused me to stumble so badly, now sounded quite generous!

I said, "Yes, I would like that!" far more forcefully than I had said it about being killed.

He warned me strictly to use this awesome anointing in great humility. The Lord cautioned me, *"You must never think it is 'you' or your own strength. None of it will be you."* He repeated this warning again, and stated that it would be dangerous to do otherwise. May He keep me and guard my heart in Messiah Yeshua. Amen.

I believe that at this very moment in history, the Lord is about to fulfill the Prophet Joel's astonishing word:

> *And afterward, I will pour out My Spirit on all people Your sons and daughters will prophesy, Your old men will dream dreams, Your young men will see visions. Even on my servants, both men and women, I will pour out My Spirit in those days* (Joel 2:28-29).

This great promise that He gave to me is also for a vast company of His everyday people: children and adults, male and female, Jew and Gentile, rich and poor, who are now being trained and disciplined as a resolute army of end-time apostles, prophets, pastors and teachers, lovesick worshipers and healing evangelists.

I believe that in making this astonishing promise to me, the Lord was also showing me that Joel's prophecy applies to all of God's people, and no longer just to His most prophetic individuals. Originally the gifts of prophecy, healing and miracles were only given to a few Israeli men, chosen out of the whole earth. The Lord wanted me to know that for ordinary believers like me, this supernatural power would be given freely. As in the Book of Acts, the air will be electric with faith and miracles. Our Lord told His disciples, "Greater works than these will you do" (John 14:12).

His Broken Heart for Israel

After a period of discussion about several topics, the Lord Yeshua abruptly said one word to me: *"Israel."* To my dismay, He began to cry, brokenhearted over the unbelief of His people. I sensed He would like me to comfort Him, and I felt unprepared and at a loss as to what to do or say.

I knelt gingerly at the Lord's feet and began to make a poor attempt to comfort Him. I said, "Lord, we are a stubborn and ignorant people. We do not know or appreciate who You are, and what You have done for us. You did everything for Your people, and we can't even call You by Your rightful name! We are a foolish, blind people, and we must come back to You and acknowledge Your Messiahship and Your sacrifice. We must come to know You, Lord." I kissed His cheek, touched His face, and kissed His feet.

I then put on His lap the little stuffed kitten which Katya had given me on my birthday as a "baby present" from Yeshua. As mentioned in the first chapter, He gave me this kitten to signify that He valued the day of my birth. As I placed this stuffed animal on His lap, I said, "Don't cry, Lord." Feeling inadequate, and wondering if giving God a stuffed animal was insulting or ridiculous, I then sat back in my rocking chair.

Please let the reader fully grasp the context of my harsh words for my own people. I deeply love and bless my own Jewish people, and will give my life on behalf of their welfare. The Lord's and my heart for the blessing and salvation of Israel and our Jewish people is fully revealed in Chapter 10, "Why Do the Nations Rage?"

The Lord's everlasting covenants to Abraham, Isaac and Jacob have never been revoked, and Paul wrote, "I have unceasing anguish in my heart for my brothers, the people of Israel." This is the Lord Yeshua's heart and this is my heart.

I have revealed here my private dialogue with my Jewish Messiah about the sin and errors of our own brothers. I pray that readers who are not of Jewish origin will never condemn or criticize the Jewish people, for whom the Lord still weeps.

My confessions to the Lord of our guilt are part of a "family argument" between believing and unbelieving Jews, and our Jewish Messiah is an integral part of that family. I always include myself in these confessions, as did the prophet Daniel, rather than pointing an accusing finger at "them." These are my kith and kin from whom I sprang, and I love them dearly.

As will be studied in the final chapter, the Church has a God-ordained responsibility to bless Israel, love her, pray for her physical safety and spiritual salvation, and honor the spiritual root of the Christian faith.

In "comforting" the Lord Jesus, I made a statement concerning His rightful name; this was a reference to the name by which He is called by the secular and religious population of Israel, which does not yet acknowledge Him as Messiah and Lord. To my enormous shame and grief, the majority of my people in Israel call Him by an abbreviated version of "Yeshua" which was coined by Jewish leaders in the few hundred years following His death. This incomplete name is an acronym which stands for: "May His memory be blotted out." I cannot adequately express the pain it causes my heart to write about this, but it is indeed the truth. I pray almost daily that His rightful and glorious name will be restored in the land and uttered with love and reverence by His Jewish brothers and sisters.

There are, of course, many believers in Israel, among whom are Jews, Arabs and non-Jewish believers from the nations who have felt called to connect deeply to the land and the people of Israel. These believers call Him by His true and wonderful name, "Yeshua," which means "Salvation."

At that time, I did not receive feedback from the Lord on my attempt to comfort Him. However, as He was departing from the coffee talk, He picked up the kitten and held it in His arms, close to His face. As He held it up, it no longer appeared to be a kitten, but seemed to have become a little lamb. He walked out, still holding it.

In order that there is no misunderstanding in this story, let me plainly state that the Lord did not physically remove the kitten from my room. As I watched Him hold it, I was no longer aware of the kitten on the bed, but after the Lord departed, it remained on the bed where I had laid it.

Later that day, I knelt and told the Lord I was sorry my attempt to comfort Him was so pitiful, and that I knew He was disappointed in me.

The Lord simply replied, *"I was not disappointed."*

Store the Word in Your Heart

During a conversation about many matters, the Lord Yeshua initiated the following challenge to me. It is extremely critical and relevant for all of His people to know and practice:

"Does My Word live in your heart?"

"Yes," I replied.

"Do you carry My Word to everyone you speak to?"

"Yes."

"Do you talk about My Word all the time?"

Again, my answer was, "Yes."

The Lord then spoke the following: *My Word is a treasure stored in your heart. It is like a library, from which you can take a book off the shelf anytime you need. Store My Word, My logos and all of My rhema words. Learn them and store them in your heart. My Word will carry you through that dark time when I AM hard to find or cannot be found.*

"I will give you an overcoming spirit, the overcoming anointing you have

prayed for; it was good to pray for that. But My Word will carry you. Satan cannot take anything from you that you have stored in your heart. He can harass you, torment you, even send beasts to devour you, but he cannot touch My Word stored in your heart.

"It is a storehouse like Joseph's storehouse of grain. Store more and more, and when the "famine" comes, go get the bread, get the grain, get the food. It will sustain you in the final battle. Every preparation you have made in your heart for the final battle with fear, will be there in your heart when the battle comes. Store it, learn it, meditate and memorize it. Keep it, and it will keep you when My Spirit does not seem to be there for you. I AM with you, but I will be in your storehouse in that day. I love you and will keep you. Amen."

The Lord then spoke to me about my current ministry and continuing assignment to feed His mature sheep. As I teach from His Word, and as He continues to give me fresh and living bread each day, I share each crumb and loaf of bread immediately with His flock.

The Lord then continued by disclosing more to me about the special friendship I have with Katya and the connected fabric of our futures and destinies. This will be discussed in the next chapter on Covenant Friendship.

The Feast of Pentecost

On the day of Pentecost, 2006, I taught on the Book of Ruth in a wonderful, Spirit-filled church in my region. This book is a true, historical account of covenant friendship, redemption, restoration and God's plan to graft the god-fearing Gentiles into His Messianic covenants. Even so, it also contains a parable of the end-time Church and Israel. The essence of this message will be explained in the final chapter on Israel.

After this teaching session, we began the main service, and entered into a time of corporate worship. On this occasion, the worship was exceptionally free and joyful, due to the blessing of the biblical Feast of *Shavuot*, meaning "weeks" in the Hebrew Scriptures. In Greek, this day is called Pentecost, which means "fifty." This is because the feast occurs fifty days after Passover.

It is also the day that the Holy Spirit was poured out on the early Jewish disciples in the Book of Acts, in keeping with the meaning of the festival, which is the wheat harvest and "firstfruits."

After an hour of zealous and extravagant worship, we settled down for announcements and the preaching of the Word. However, the Lord took me into His presence, and I did not resurface until the service was nearly over.

The Secret Place of the Most High

During the coffee talk which took place on the day after Pentecost, I was discussing with the Lord this particular manifestation of His presence which I was feeling in church. It was exactly how I had felt in the service in 2004, when His presence returned to me after a long, dry season. I began to describe to the Lord the four "versions" of His presence I have identified thus far in my life, and how each one has a unique quality, characteristic and response from me. I believe there are many other expressions of His inexhaustible and glorious reality, but these are the four I have known to this point.

First, there is a reverent awe and fear of the holiness of God. In this atmosphere, I am perfectly still, barely breathing, and in the words of the Apostle John, "like a dead man." This seems to me the most fearful manifestation because His holiness produces enormous discomfort in the flesh of any sinful person. The Hebrew word for glory is *kavod*, which means "weightiness." His glorious presence incapacitates me with such pressure that I am unable to speak. I am undone and afraid, but do not want it to end. I am conflicted, for there is no relaxation or comfort possible in this atmosphere, and yet to reject it would be like leaving the ocean to splash in a dirty puddle in the alley. It was this holy fear of the Lord that Satan attempted to counterfeit in the visitation of thick dread which awakened me out of a deep sleep.

Second, there is the excited activity of the Holy Spirit, described in Chapter 4 ("God's Glory Returns"). This is the sense of being filled to overflowing with an unseen source of "breath," and feeling a good deal of muscular activity associated with tension and the subsequent release of pressure. It can feel like sobbing without tears and heaving without sorrow. It is as if my flesh cannot contain the energy or activity of His Spirit. In my limited understanding, this seems to occur when the Lord is particularly pleased or excited about something and is dramatically signaling me to "pay attention." When this activity occurs, I often tell my family, "He is knocking on my door." At these moments, I excuse myself and go off to be alone with Him, to determine why He is seeking my attention.

Third, there is an expression which can only be described as the "chemistry of love." I must emphasize that there is no sexual element to this pleasure, and it bypasses all the obvious zones; the Lover of our Soul is not interested in our parts, but in our hearts. This expression of the Lord's great love for us is equally available to all His children, and the delight of this heavenly touch is too intimate to describe. David referred to it in Psalm 16:11 and Solomon described it in his Song of Songs. It was this holy love which Satan cynically imitated in the demonic experience in Birmingham, which I wryly call, "The Night of the Living Bed."

Fourth, there is the manifestation which I experienced in church on Pentecost and at the anointed service in 2004. I have also entered it a number of times in my basement, when we prayed and worshiped on Shabbat. It feels as if I am surrounded by an unseen bubble or cocoon, which provides impenetrable shielding and safety. Sights and sounds around us seem to disappear, although our senses are fully functioning. As I described to Him this invisible encasement, He told me, *"This is the secret place of the Most High"* (Psalm 91). This is the place of abiding in Him and hiding "under the shadow of His wings." This is a place of security in times of great danger, when no physical shelter will offer trustworthy protection. We must learn to cultivate being in the "hiding place" now, in a time of relative safety, for when the trouble comes upon us, it will too late to learn the art of hiding in a non-physical shelter. Even unbelievers know that, in one hour an entire city could be destroyed, even a nation. Such is the age in which we live.

There is something else I have experienced on rare occasions, which I believe is a variation on "The secret place of the Most High," but it might be a different expression of His Spirit. This is a sensation of heavy, dreamlike tranquility, as if by anesthesia. The Lord has covered me this way two or three times when I was in severe emotional pain, the kind which actually hurts in the area of the physical heart. His presence immediately covers and removes all emotional pain, and even when it departs, the pain does not return. This is like a blanket of mercy on a raw heart.

This sensation also occurred once during a coffee talk; as I began to speak to the Lord in my normal way, I was enveloped in this sweet dreaminess which suppressed my ability to speak, almost as with a medication. This feels so wonderful that I'm not surprised the Lord does not do this very often; it could become habit-forming, and should come with a warning label!

Perhaps I am not meant to categorize every aspect of the inexhaustible resources of His Spirit, but rather to just receive and enjoy each type of visitation with which He chooses to bless me.

After I had reviewed with the Lord these four types of His Presence, He added some information about a fifth type, which I have heard about, but for reasons which will immediately become obvious, I have never experienced. He spoke to me about "The Martyr's Grace."

"The martyr's grace is like the secret place of the Most High, but it is not as peaceful because they are busy attacking your body. There is no chance for 'peace of mind.' But the martyr's grace gives you a resolve and strength, so that you do not go into panic and fear, like a shrieking, flailing animal, wild with panic.

"This is how people die without the martyr's grace: Panic, pain, terror and wild desperation consume them. With Me, there is still groaning and moaning with

pain and sadness, still suffering, but you have a resolve to endure without panic or shrieking because you are waiting patiently for your spirit to depart, when you know the pain will stop. You look forward to the departure of your spirit, and this gives you peace, hope and resolve."

In my human fear and limited understanding, I can only hope that the martyr's grace has some components of the holy "anesthesia" manifestation described above. As I make every effort not to fear the painful process of death, I take comfort in hoping that some of the agony would be partially diminished in this dreamlike presence of the Spirit of God.

The Sin of Judging

On one occasion, I had given a teaching on the sin of judging and tearing down other believers. I shared a powerful word about how terrible it will be for us on the Day of Judgment if we have condemned our brothers and sisters in our hearts or criticized them.

Several days later, an incident occurred which involved several people I knew. There was a severe disagreement between two people about an issue, and I was very upset with one of them because of his views.

A friend called me, and we began discussing this problem. Before I knew it, I heard myself making a sarcastic remark about the one with whom I disagreed. The phone call ended soon after that, with both of us agreeing to pray about the situation.

Later that afternoon, I was thinking about my sarcastic remark, and how pointed it was. As I thought about the situation, I found myself getting angrier and angrier at the person. Oddly, I was not trying to work up anger, and I scarcely perceived the snare into which I was stepping. The anger grew so strong that it seemed to have a life of its own.

An unfamiliar darkness began to consume my spirit, and I felt as if I were falling into an abyss which separated me from God. I tried with all of my effort to pull myself out of this condition, making a deliberate attempt to think good thoughts about God and the person who had upset me. I could do nothing, so strong was the grip of darkness.

I realized that if I were to stay in this condition, I could never teach the Bible again. In fact, I could never go to church and worship God again. At the risk of being theologically controversial, I realized that if I stayed in this condition, I could not enter the Kingdom of heaven. I was terrified by my own sin and felt irrevocably trapped. I then felt the Holy Spirit say to me, "*Listen to the tape of your teaching on judging.*"

I began to play the tape and listen to what should have been a very familiar voice…my own. The strangest sensation took place: the voice I was hearing was full of anointing and righteous zeal; it issued the strictest warning about judging others. The voice was so foreign and unfamiliar that I actually felt that I was listening to someone else! I was irritated with the woman on the tape because what she was saying was in direct contrast to my state of mind. Obviously, I realized it was me, but it didn't seem like me.

Then I began to let her words wash over me and sink into my diseased spirit. I began to feel conviction from the Holy Spirit, and this produced a growing sense of genuine repentance. As the Word of God was preached, it did its awesome work of healing, repentance and restoration.

Despite knowing the identity of the speaker, I asked the Lord in astonishment, "Who is this woman?" His answer was not complimentary.

"She is the opposite of you."

By this I understood that my regenerate nature and my sin nature were so completely opposite, that the gap between them was like the incalculable chasm between heaven and hell, impossible to traverse. The version of me which was walking in His Spirit brought words of life and repentance. The version of me which walked according to the deeds of the flesh brought darkness and death. (Rom. 7:21-25).

> *The one who sows to please his sinful nature, from that nature will reap destruction; the one who sows to please the Spirit, from the Spirit will reap eternal life* (Gal. 6:8).

> *The acts of the sinful nature are obvious: sexual immorality, impurity and debauchery; idolatry and witchcraft; hatred, discord, jealousy, fits of rage, selfish ambition, dissentions, factions and envy; drunkenness, orgies and the like. I warn you, as I did before, those who live like this will not inherit the Kingdom of God* (Gal. 5:19-21).

As the Lord said to Cain, when he was angry at his brother:

> *Why are you angry? Why is your face downcast? If you do what is right, will you not be accepted? But if you do not do what is right, sin is crouching at your door; it desires to have you, but you must master it* (Gen. 4:6-7).

When I opened the door to sin, by indulging myself with that satisfying sarcastic remark, sin achieved its foothold in me; I became powerless to stem the tide of increasing darkness. If I had submitted to the Holy Spirit during the phone call, the door would have been closed to sin; I would have mastered it rather than been overcome. May I remember this terrible lesson and never open the door to sin again. A small breach will become a chasm of eternal regret.

The Sin of Abortion

In Chapter 4, I referred to a series of repentance conferences which a group of intercessors and I have attended; these are sponsored by World for Jesus Ministries, led by an upright and humble woman of God, Nita Johnson.[11] Through these difficult meetings, the Lord has called for His church to weep deeply and repent on behalf of our nation, for the shedding of innocent blood on American soil. Over the last seven years, Nita has been directed by the Lord to repent for a number of monumental sins which we, as a nation, have committed; in the same way, the prophet Daniel repented for the sins of his nation despite the fact that he personally had not committed these sins.

Earlier conferences had covered our crimes of treachery, broken treaties and the slaughter of the First Nations people. Later, intercessors covered the brutal exploitation of kidnapped African slaves whose blood and tears built the economy of our young nation. Following slavery, we wept for the cruel and shameful treatment of freed slaves during the one-hundred year period between the Emancipation Proclamation and the Civil Rights movement, known as the "Jim Crow Era." Finally, in the most recent conferences, we began to address the hidden, lucrative and highly politicized world of abortion: the destruction of the most innocent and helpless members of society, the unborn children.[12]

Several gatherings have been devoted to the repentance and intercession needed to stop this atrocity which continues to this day. I have attended four of these conferences and will comment briefly on two which addressed abortion; one was in Jacksonville and the other in Atlanta, both during 2006. The intercessors who attended were willing to enter the gruesome and medically hidden world of the abortion clinic and learn the truth about this horrific practice.

We were shown films in which doctors and nurses testified that their consciences can no longer allow them to continue to practice abortion. What they had previously believed was mere "tissue" in earlier years, before accurate intrauterine photography and advanced fetology were available, they now believe is a human baby, indistinguishable from other babies in form, features and feelings. The conscience-saving pretense that the fetus is an amorphous blob of cells has been stripped away. The baby in the womb can now be clearly seen with its heartbeat, brainwaves and thumb-sucking, as can the hauntingly recognizable remains after the procedure is finished.

Women who have undergone abortions also testified on these films. They said that they were not properly informed by the doctor or clinic staff as to the nature, size or development of the unborn child within them. They were not shown any accurate material on what happens to the unborn child during an abortion or what the child looks like. They could not see what the doctor saw as they lay on the operating table. Had they seen, they would have not gone through with this irrevocable act. These poor women have lived with unspeakable regret ever since, and their grief was heartrending.

In one of the sessions we saw an older film called "The Silent Scream." It was an excellent documentary hosted by Dr. Bernard Nathanson,[13] who gave detailed medical explanations of the procedure while showing footage available in the 1980s. This film relied on ultrasound technology and displayed gray and pulsating images of the unborn child and its removal from the womb. This shadowy imagery made the procedure appear less stark than the astounding uterine photography available today. Nevertheless, even with ultrasound, one could clearly see the unborn baby scream and pull violently away as the instruments of destruction approached his body.

A more recent film by Dr. Nathanson is called "Eclipse of Reason" and shows the grotesque reality of a "late abortion," medically defined as second or third trimester. I will not describe the horror of what we saw. If America could see what really happens, the nation would arise with one voice and say, "No more! Never again!" This is the cry of our Jewish people about our own holocaust.

Dr. Nathanson was formerly an abortionist. In 1969, he was co-founder of the National Abortion Rights Action League. He was also the former director of New York's City's Center for Reproductive and Sexual Health, then the largest abortion clinic in the world. During this time, he presided over 60,000 abortions.

In the late 1970s he turned against abortion to become a prominent pro-life advocate, arguing that the advances in the science of fetology make it impossible to deny the humanity of the unborn. Dr. Nathanson is currently Clinical Associate Professor of Obstetrics and Gynecology at New York Medical College and a visiting scholar at Vanderbilt University.[14]

After watching the film, the intercessors entered into a period of grieving and crying out for this slaughter to be stopped. We were aware that the God of Life would not leave the blood of the innocent unavenged, and that our nation would pay a price too great to bear if this legalized murder is not overturned.

As the weeping began in the Jacksonville conference, I had difficulty connecting to the true impact and reality of abortion. I wept a little, but it was not proportionate to the necessary level of repentance. I had been instructed by the Spirit of the Lord that when I could not produce tears, I was to sigh and moan over wickedness, as taught in Ezekiel 9:3-6. After some time, He gave me the grace to weep, but I knew I had not contributed enough to the "cup of tears" on that day.

In the next session, we saw a six-minute film called "Hard Truth."[15] It is a high-quality video depicting the inescapable carnage and hideous reality of abortion. As I forced my eyes to watch the perfectly filmed "real-time" abortion, as well as the bodies and body parts of well-developed babies, I went into severe shock and trauma. I have never gone to see a "horror movie," where the screen is gratuitously littered with blood and body parts. As I watched this legal and medically acceptable procedure unfold before me, I began to involuntarily scream and gasp in horror and for the next half-hour was wracked with trembling and breathless sobs. A darkness and hopelessness entered my soul as scenes continued of heads and arms, faces, feet and decaying perfect bodies strewn across the screen, mostly pulled out of trash cans. My soul was more traumatized than in my visits to the Holocaust Museums, both the one in Washington, D.C. and the one in Jerusalem, Israel called *Yad Vashem*.

This film helped the intercessors to grasp the reality of the hidden activities of the clinic. It was not difficult to fill up the cup of tears on that day. The weeping among us was devastating, although it was actually a small amount compared to the scope of this national guilt.

After some time had elapsed, perhaps close to an hour of anguish, I personally began to feel a tangible blanket of peace and comfort descend on me from the Lord. I knew that the others would soon begin to feel the same relief, but I believe He gave me this peace at the precise moment that He knew my soul could not bear any more pain. I felt His manifested presence wrapping me in a cocoon of love, and the grief and pain were miraculously swallowed up, as if receiving anesthesia. It was the sweet hiding place called "The secret place of the Most High."

Soon afterward, His Spirit comforted all of His weeping children, for He never sends us out of a repentance session carrying grief and depression with us. It is not in His character to leave us in this broken state; after the work of repentance is complete, He is pleased to comfort us and give us His joy and peace.

If one cannot bear to look upon these graphic and accurate films, one should never again be silent until this grisly practice is abolished, and the shedding of innocent blood is finally halted!

There Is Forgiveness!

I must close this section with the Father's tender heart of love and forgiveness for any of His daughters who have had abortions. These repentance gatherings include times of prayer and ministry to women who need to receive and fully experience His healing, mercy and complete restoration. For such a one to even attend a conference of this nature takes enormous courage and humility, since she will be subjected to graphic video presentations of what is truly happening in this procedure. For her to then come forward publicly for prayer and healing takes an even greater degree of courage and exposure.

I never knew or understood that the unborn was a true and well-developed baby until later in my walk with the Lord. I was influenced by attitudes of denial, self-serving convenience and selfishness which stayed with me long after my salvation. It was only by Yeshua's mercies that I was spared such an agonizing decision as many have faced. Full restoration is available, and the Lord will wipe away every tear and all guilt from His children's lives; His heart of love is inexhaustible.

I pray before our merciful High Priest Jesus Christ that nothing I have written in this section will produce any guilt or condemnation for any of my precious sisters who have, for various reasons, aborted an unborn child. We are all sinners and lawbreakers before His holy standards, and we are equally dependent on His sinless blood to make atonement for our souls. If not for the grace of God, any one of us could have done this thing in ignorance, fear or desperation. The Father's blessing and Yeshua's faithful mercy be yours, now and forever! Amen.

A Vision of His Love

In the evening sessions, we worshiped with great intensity, and heard outstanding teachings on holiness, humility and the glory of God returning to His house. Each evening, the presence of God grew stronger and carried us into new depths of His love and power. By Thursday evening, as the worship ended and Nita began teaching on humility, I was completely overcome with His glory and was unable to move for at least an hour.

In the morning session on the last day, we interceded for America with tears of repentance and supplication, to push back the severe judgments that our sins have brought upon us. The subject of the coming judgments upon America would be the subject of another book. Much material is available to God's people, warning them with great detail about this unpopular truth, and one excellent source of information can be found at The Prophecy Club.[16]

As the time of repentance was ending, I saw in a vision a burnt offering. It consisted of wood, smoke and fire, but no animal was laid upon the altar because the Sacrificed Lamb has been slain, once for all time and once for all sins. I had only seen such an offering in a vision once before, at a special yearly prayer meeting called "Day to Pray for the Peace of Jerusalem," which occurs on the first Sunday in October and is sponsored by Eagles' Wings Ministries, under the leadership of Robert Stearns.[17] Both in the previous vision and in the one occurring as we repented for America, I knew that the Lord was pleased with our sacrifice, and I could see the smoke rising up to Him as a sweet offering which was acceptable to Him.

From the moment I saw this scene, I received an increasingly strong visitation of the Lord's presence, and no more weeping was possible for me. Others continued repenting for a little while longer, but I was already entering another realm. As I sat in this powerful presence, I felt Yeshua very close to my face. I heard Him say, "*I AM in your face, right here,*" and at that moment I saw Him, although my eyes were closed.

The Lord Yeshua moved back a pace and placed His hands on either side of my arms, giving me a little "squeeze." He shook His head, and with a mixture of tenderness and frustration asked, "*Do you have any idea how much I love you?*"

I wanted to answer correctly, so I said, "Yes." Then I realized I did not know how much He loved me, so I quickly changed my answer to "No." Then I decided I really had no idea of the measure of His love; my final answer was, "I don't know."

The Lord then spread out His tallit in front of Himself and said, "*Come here, I just want to wrap you in this.*" He held me close, tightly wrapped up in His prayer shawl for quite a while, with my head resting against Him. I felt loved and safe, and did not want the hug to end. Finally, He released me.

The Lord then stretched out His hands as far as they could go to either side, still holding the edges of His tallit with each hand. As He stretched them out, I could see the marks on His hands. Of course, it appeared to be the position of His arms during the crucifixion, and I knew this extraordinary gesture of love had a double meaning.

He said, "*I love you this much,*" as a Father would say to his little girl, showing her his great big arms of love. Then the Lord smiled and laughed. He continued, "*Why are you always so surprised when I show you favor and kindness? Don't act surprised anymore. This is an outgrowth of My great love, My favor and My kindness. You should not be surprised; just be glad and rejoice. This is how I treat those whom I favor.*" (See Esther 6:9.)

Before I share the third expression of love which our dearest Savior extended to me, I need to explain one little quirk in my personality. For as long as I can remember, I have kissed the backs of people's hands. It is mostly limited to times of ministry, and is never premeditated. This loving expression is fully spontaneous, as fleeting as a butterfly alighting and immediately forgotten as I move on to my next spiritual assignment.

My parents told me I once kissed the hand of a young black waiter in a southern restaurant when I was a very little girl. During the racially biased environment of the 1950s, this was an awkward moment for the poor man and formy parents, but no harm came of it. I never thought about the Lord's per-

spective on this behavior, nor did I realize He was paying attention to such a tiny gesture.

Yeshua took my hands in His, and kissed them a number of times, perhaps three times. He said, *"You love to kiss people's hands. I love to kiss your hands, too. They are sweet hands."* Sensing that this marvelous visit was drawing to a close, I took His hands in mine and kissed them. He told me that He was looking forward to our next coffee talk when I returned home from this trip. We had missed quite a few coffee talks due to the conditions of traveling. The Lord knew that I was sad that He was leaving, and He said, *"I never leave; I just come in different forms and ways at differing times."* He then released me to my waiting friends, and I began to regain my normal strength very quickly.

About a week later, the Lord spoke to me more about the unchanging nature of His love. He used urgent and emphatic language to press upon me the importance of grasping the full measure of His unchanging and unwavering love for me. He reminded me of the extraordinary gestures of love He showed me in Jacksonville, and explained why He did all that:

"You must know my love. The work I have called you to do is hard, lonely work. If you don't know My love better at this season, the work will be too much for you. I AM telling you ahead of time. Come into the full understanding of My love now! Now, Jill. This moment, this coffee talk, and never let go of it again!"

I heard His tone grow increasingly loud and forceful.

"I AM shouting at you! Can you hear Me?"

The Lord then took on the impression of a leading man in an old Bette Davis movie, where the neurotic wife is being a silly goose, and someone must talk some sense into her! In a humorous moment of high drama, He grabbed my shoulders and cried, *"I love you, you fool!"*

My dear Yeshua then added quietly, *"Do I make Myself clear?"*

He made me promise I would never doubt His love again. I am reluctant to promise the Lord things that I have no confidence I will be faithful to keep. However, in the rare event that He extracts a promise from me, He will not take "no." Therefore, I gave Him my sacred promise with fear and trembling.

The Pattern of His Progressive Revelations

As I review the amazing path I have traveled with the Lord God since His glory returned to me in 2004, I began to see a pattern emerge. I couldn't see it until recently, as the puzzle pieces began to fit.

I believe that every Christian can benefit from this outline, despite the fact that we are each unique, and His plan for each son or daughter is tailored for the specific blueprint of each life. Nevertheless, there are universal principles about the Lord which are of great value to His children. Here is what I have observed:

First, the Lord put a restlessness and longing in my heart to know His presence and dwell in His glory. I was seized with a holy discontent, and the normal American Christian life became painfully unsatisfying to me. My parched soul cried out, "There must be something more!" (Psalm 42:2)

This restlessness lasted many years. Even so, the sovereign God showed me that the eleven "dry" years were not silent years, and that He was very much at work in my life during those years. The Lord is not pleased when I refer to those years as a waste of time or lacking significant growth. He sees things differently, and He has reassured me that He had a great purpose to work out in that period (Rom. 8:28).

Second, our Lord drew me into the practice of worshiping Him in Spirit and in truth. This included loving Him with all my heart, soul and strength, according to Deuteronomy. My worship utilized my mind, will and emotions, and I learned to extol God through Scriptural prayers and utterances. The Lord Yeshua taught me the discipline of putting aside my own self-centered need for good music and entertainment. I learned to focus all of my attention on giving to the Lord what He deserves and declaring to our Maker His own attributes (John 4:23).

Third, the Lord taught me, through wonderful teachers and prophets, "the art of waiting on God." I believe that He was pleased when I began waiting on Him, and He immediately began to shower me, and sometimes deluge me, with a visitation of His glory. This daily experience showed me an awesome and incapacitating side of His presence I had never known. There were many occasions over a six-month period that I sat in this powerful glory, often without words, visions or revelations. The Presence of Almighty God alone was more than satisfying (Psalm 130:5; Isa. 40:31).

Fourth, the Lord Yeshua called me aside to spend three days with Him, cut off from all support and contact. He allured me into the desert, so that I would fall in love with Him.

Therefore, I am now going to allure her; I will lead her into the desert and speak tenderly to her... There she will sing as in the days of her youth, As in the day she came up out of Egypt. "In that day," declares the Lord, "you will call Me 'my husband'; you will no longer call me 'my master'" (Hos. 2:14-16).

At the end of my three days, the Lord Jesus declared me to be in love with Him, and it was so! He took me away into the desert, and with every prop and distraction removed, I finally fell in love with my Messiah and Savior.

During the same period, the Lord tested and refined my trust in His goodness by revealing to me the way I would glorify Him in my death. He held out to me a bitter cup and asked me if I was willing to drink it. In fact, He asked me if I "would like" to drink it, which exposed my unbelief and mistrust of His goodness and His plans for me. The Lord Yeshua allowed the sins of fear, resentment and unbelief to surface in my daily thoughts. Attitudes that were hidden were now plainly exposed by the revelation of my martyrdom and the circumstances surrounding it (Matt. 20:22).

Fifth, the Lord showed me the full measure of His love after I had fully submitted to His plans and purposes for my life. I was not ready to understand His love until I had known the cost of discipleship. He strongly emphasized that if I did not grasp His unshakable love for me, I would not be able to do the difficult work He has prepared for me (John 13:1; Rom. 8:35).

Sixth, God began to reveal that to walk in His perfect plan would produce great joy in me. It is a delight to do the very work one was created to do! This piece of the puzzle appears in the following coffee talk testimony.

From Melancholy to Joy

In this particular dialogue, the Lord was asking me why I am sad so much of the time. I attempted to explain my reasons, but ended up admitting I had no idea. He suggested that I "miss Him" even though He is actually present at all times, because I don't ever have as much of the Lord Yeshua as I crave. After telling me that it is good to long for heaven, He instructed me with these words:

"But the work I have given you, laid out for you, is designed to bring you joy—full joy, unspeakable joy. You were made for this work at this moment in your history, in My history, and in the world's history.

"You are entering the moment you were designed and created for! I AM excited. The work I have prepared is hard, but My work was hard and yet it brought Me joy to do My Father's will, day after day after day. You will be the same. I really don't want you to be so sad so much of the time...Do not dread the hard work I have prepared for you. It is delightful to do the very work I have created for you to do.

"I love you, Jill. You are a good and obedient daughter to Me. You bring Me joy and pleasure. I know that you love Me. You are not perfect, but you are being made ready, and you are very close to being prepared for the work I have for you. Keep pressing in and waiting on Me, and do not get discouraged."

Thus, the larger pattern of the Lord's progressive revelations toward me can be more easily understood, by examining the order in which they were given. In summary, they consist of: 1) the discontent of a restless soul; 2) worshiping in Spirit and in truth; 3) the power of His glory; 4) the extravagant devotion of a lovesick bride; 5) the offer and acceptance of the bitter cup; 6) Messiah's incomparable love revealed; 7) the joy of doing the work for which He designed us.

The Sins of Pride and Presumption

I was teaching a series of lessons on the glory of God. During one particular lesson, I explained a phenomenon I had noticed over time: sometimes I can feel the Lord's glory when I am sitting in an anointed conference. I shared that as various speakers pray or preach, I feel an increase or decrease of His glorious presence, depending on what they say or pray. I also conveyed that I felt a higher level of His glory in an atmosphere of repentance than in an atmosphere of excitement and celebration.

Although these were true statements, I added something more: I stated that by perceiving this "barometer" of His glory, I could determine the Lord's level of participation or pleasure in what was happening at a particular conference. Little did I know that I had just crossed a dangerous line.

Later that day, I listened to this teaching on CD and found nothing objectionable. I was vaguely aware that I could not feel the Lord's presence for the remainder of that day and that when I knelt to pray before bed, I felt strangely "alone." However, feelings are not to be trusted or consulted, and I simply assumed that "I won't always feel Him, but I just press on in faith." This is a healthy attitude toward the unreliability of feelings, but it turns out something really was wrong, and I was clueless.

At 2:00 a.m. I had a very short dream. I saw a white toilet, perfectly clean. I then saw an unseen hand lift up the toilet seat to expose the rim underneath. It was abominably filthy, with dark splotches of unspeakable growth. I was appalled and immediately started searching for the bottle of bleach. My motivation to scrub the repugnant rim was intense. At that moment I woke up with a terrible, sinking feeling.

I writhed in bed, crying out to the Lord, "Please, let that *not* be me! Let that be anyone or anything but me! Please tell me that's not me, Lord!"

The Lord instantly played back for me that one sentence from my teaching where I had implied that I could determine His opinion about a meeting by my perception of the level of His glory. I heard my words with a new perspective as He played back this sentence. He then said, *"This is pride and presumption."*

Without further explanation, I understood that no sinful human can presume to understand or measure His glory, nor can we use it to pass judgments on His people or their activities. I got out of bed, and knelt down to repent of my sin. While I was sincere in my repentance, I was aware that I did not weep over my pride but felt some genuine discomfort about it. I then went back to bed and heard the Lord say, *"How can I trust you with My power if you can't be trusted to stay humble with these very small things?"*

The next morning happened to be a scheduled coffee talk. I talked to the Lord Yeshua about the incident and expressed my sorrow over my pride and presumption. I wasn't sure what else to say.

He said, *"You haven't cried yet."*

I asked the Lord to help me cry over this, since I was afraid I could not produce sufficient repentance to cry. I knelt at His feet, and He immediately gave me tears of genuine repentance. I asked my Lord not to withdraw His glory or His presence from me, or to withhold the gifts and power He had promised me. I told Him, "I cannot bear to be apart from Your glory and Your presence and love and power." Then I returned to my chair and waited.

The Lord then spoke to me: *"You have not earned My glory, Jill. I do reward you according to the cleanness of your hands and heart. This is a delicate balance to maintain."*

This statement confused me and I thought, "This is too hard for me." Then I wondered if He would withhold His glory from me because of my pride.

The Lord said, *"No, I might send My glory to expose your pride. At times, My glory can kill someone. My glory killed Uzzah and Nadav and Abihu. My anger is connected to the power of My glory and holiness. Wrath and glory are connected in My coming judgments and My return to wage war"* (see Lev. 10:1-3; 2 Sam. 6:6-7).

I thanked Yeshua for the cross, through which I knew I could be restored to fellowship with Him. The Lord then reassured me that He would not withhold any good thing from me, due to His great love and faithfulness. He reminded me to always put on the "Cloak of Humility," spoken of in the awesome book by Rick Joyner, *The Call*.[18] The Lord reminded me how subtle and swift is pride to come out of my mouth, and how I don't even feel it happening. He added, *"You must walk very low to receive what I have for you."*

I thanked the Lord, and thought this was finished. But He asked me, *"Do you love Me?"*

I answered, "Yes, I love you so much. You are everything to me."

The Lord continued, *"Do you trust in My great love, despite this transgression?"*

I replied, "Yes, I trust in Your great love. You do not withdraw Your love."

The Lord was not satisfied. *"I sense you are not fully trusting in My love, even though you are confessing it with your mouth, which is right. Is this in your heart, or only in your mouth?"*

I searched my heart and made a choice to trust in His unfailing love with all my heart. He had rightly perceived that I still felt that He was angry at me for my pride. As I did this, I wept before Him.

I told Him, "Last night when I prayed, it didn't even occur to me that something was wrong. I didn't know to ask You if I had done anything to displease You."

His answer came with an affectionate smile. *"No, I had to wake you up and tell you!"*

I knew that even the disgusting dream was His goodness to me and answered, "Thank You, that was Your kindness. Thank You for loving me so much that You would not leave me separated from You, not even knowing what I had done."

We were fully restored to the joy of our great love for each other, and the coffee talk ended soon after. I praise Him for revealing my sin to me so that fellowship could be restored. The price of holding onto sin is too unbearable, and forgiveness and restoration are always available through His sacrifice and His lovingkindness (Psalm 51).

Do You love Me? Do You Trust Me?

In the previous testimony, notice that the Lord asked me, "Do you love Me?" When I replied that I did, He continued, "Do you trust in My great love, despite this transgression?"

There is a big difference between what we mean by "love," and what the Lord Jesus counts as our "love" for Him. There were many times over the last ten months when I would pour out my heart of love to the Lord. I expressed my love for Him with great feeling and depth, with genuine words and many tears, with true and deep emotions from my heart. This was good and pleasing to Him.

Even so, the Lord plainly told me that while my emotional love for Him was at a maximum level, He would begin to measure my love for Him by my level of trust in His goodness. Yeshua explained that trusting in His goodness, in His character, in His loving motivations behind everything He does and says, is the most important measuring line of our love for Him. The emotions are fine, but they will not hold us in the day of trouble.

He shared with me that it will get harder and harder to trust in His goodness as lawlessness increases and very bad things happen to His people. This will be fully explained in the final section of this chapter entitled, "The Love of Most Will Grow Cold."

Even when life is relatively calm and easy, it is sometimes hard for me to trust in His goodness. When I sinned against Him in the section above, I continued to feel that He was still angry with me, even after I had repented. The Lord had to tell me that I was not fully trusting in His great love. How much harder will it be when the "tree is dry"?

Let each one who loves Yeshua the Messiah begin to focus on trusting in the excellence of His character. Everything He does is for our good and our benefit, even when our minds tell us otherwise. This will prove to be the end-times test for all believers: Do we trust in His goodness?

The Faith of Children

In August of 2006 I had a dream at midnight. It was a particular type of dream I have had twice before, and I call it a "power dream." This is hard for me to describe, but I mean that throughout the entire dream, the strong power of God is manifesting upon my body as I sleep. This power is so overwhelming that I tremble and almost cringe in my bed, as I feel His visitation accompanying the events of the dream.

In this dream, I was observing a prayer meeting at my church, consisting only of children. There were about six or seven children, boys and girls, ranging from ages five to eleven. The children were not seated nor standing in a circle; rather, they were standing, "stationed" at various positions around the sanctuary, and were saying very little.

As an observer, I knew certain things about this situation. First, I understood that the Lord Yeshua Himself was present at this meeting, and I could see Him with the eyes of my spirit. I also knew that none of the children could see Him but were all acutely aware of His presence and location in the church at all times. The children were praying intensely in silence for long periods of time. At some point, one of them would utter a brief prayer, often just a single sentence. This one sentence was so powerful that the Lord's response was tremendous. My body, lying in bed, could feel the strength of His response and pleasure at each child's prayer.

At a certain point, the Lord addressed all the children together, in the back of the church. He needed to correct them about a certain matter, which I was able to understand at the time I was hearing it. After He corrected them, most of the children went back to their stations to continue in prayer. However, the oldest child present, a girl of about eleven, stood before the Lord, looked up at Him (though not seeing Him), and began to demand an explanation for His correction. She said something like, "I don't understand why You had to do that. Why did You correct us about that? I don't like what You said."

The Lord Yeshua just looked down at her and gave her no answer. After a few minutes, I lost track of the girl and returned my attention to the prayer meeting. Just then a boy of about nine, who was standing at the back of the church, was praying in the loudest whisper I have ever heard. His prayer was so simple, but the response it brought was astounding. He said, "I pray that everyone in this place will be filled with Your Spirit!" When I heard him pray this, I realized that the last time he had prayed was about twenty minutes ago, and he had prayed the same sentence!

As soon as the words left his mouth, I felt the power and presence of the Lord descend on the meeting, and on me in my bed. It was so strong that I instinctively curled up into a tight little ball, to reduce the impact on my body. The meeting continued in this manner.

Then I became aware of the Lord Yeshua, now standing on the platform near the pulpit. To my dismay, the girl was still standing before Him, hands on hips, and still demanding an explanation for His corrective words. I was shocked at her impudence. I knew she could not see Him at all, yet she was intently staring into His eyes, which I was permitted to see. She continued to say, "You still haven't explained to me why You did that. Tell me why You had to correct us about that. I don't understand." Yeshua gazed down at her patiently and said not a word.

At this point, I began to rebuke her in my thoughts. I said, "Be quiet, child! Do not talk to the Lord that way. He was right to correct you, and what He said was absolutely correct, and you guys needed to hear it. Leave Him alone, and go back to praying!" I did notice, however, that even when she was speaking to Him in this manner, His power did not diminish in the meeting or upon me.

As soon as I thought these judgments against her, I felt the Lord's great love for her. In my heart, I heard Him say to me, *"Look at her, staring right at Me, into My eyes, even though she cannot see Me. She has so much faith to confront Me this way. She knows I am right here. Do you know how much faith it takes to yell at Me like that? I love her faith!"*

He did not seem to be defending her defiance but was commending her for her persistence and stubbornness and her unwillingness to leave until she received her answer from Him. She got right "in His face," and this seemed to please Him more than her (in my opinion) bad attitude may have displeased Him. The dream ended there and I awoke, still in His presence.

I believe the Lord was showing me His end-time army of children, a mighty company of prayer warriors. Though their words were few, the strength of their sincerity and faith made their prayers very effectual and pleasing to the Lord's heart. They were not afraid of long periods of silence, which were just as powerful as their words.

These children were ordinary children but were radically committed to Him. They were not constrained by the normal awkwardness and "rules" of adult prayer meetings, such as praying in a circle or taking turns uttering lengthy prayers on a given topic. (I offer no criticism here, merely an observation of the habits found in many prayer meetings.)

In addition, the dreaded silence, which is so incredibly threatening to most adults, did not bother them in the least. They were busy with Him whether someone spoke or not, and they were unified, despite standing at dispersed places throughout the sanctuary. This was the most exciting prayer meeting I have ever seen! Why are we normally so bored?

The Love of Most will Grow Cold

Then you will be handed over to be persecuted and put to death, and you will be hated by all nations because of me. At that time many will turn away from the faith and will betray and hate each other, and many false prophets will appear and deceive many people. Because of the increase of wickedness [lawlessness], the love of most will grow cold, but he who stands firm to the end will be saved (Matt. 24:9-13).

The Lord has begun to speak to me about a terribly hard reality we will all have to face. Lawlessness will come upon our way of life, and His children will suffer intensely as a result of this oppression, injustice and violence. It should not seem strange to us. Large numbers of His beloved children are suffering at the hands of lawless and brutal men, as well as merciless and cruel governments, at this very moment in other parts of the globe. Likewise, His people have suffered this way throughout the pages of the Bible, and these sufferings are documented in much historical literature since the New Testament was written.

Dear friends, do not be surprised at the painful trial you are suffering, as though something strange were happening to you. But rejoice that you participate in the sufferings of Christ, so that you may be overjoyed when his glory is revealed (1 Pet. 4:12-13).

Recently, the Lord gave me a most disturbing and realistic dream in which the unthinkable happened: I was victimized by a lawless man and despite my repeated cries to the Lord to rescue me, He did not. When I awoke, the first question the Lord asked me was, *"Are you angry with Me?"*

I replied that I was not angry but was stunned and could not understand why He did not rescue me when I called upon His name for help, over and over. The Lord told me to record the dream in my journal, and then He would speak to me about it. I wrote down every painful detail and read it aloud to Jesus.

The Lord then led me to Hebrews 11 and began to speak to me about Cain and Abel, as well as the multitude of beloved saints described in this densely packed passage. Abel is commended for having faith, and Hebrews asserts that God was pleased with his offerings. We also see that Abel's testimony still speaks and lives, despite his removal from the earth at the hands of a lawless brother.

The Lord then asked me if I thought He loved Abel less than Cain because He did not rescue Abel from this lawless one with whom God was most displeased, while Cain lived for a long time after this event. I replied that the opposite was true; that I believed God loved Abel more than Cain, but nevertheless allowed him to be bludgeoned to death without rescue.

I then studied the "heroes of faith" who escaped the edge of the sword, did not burn in the flames, were not devoured by fierce beasts, had miraculous victories over enemies and armies too strong for them, and even experienced resurrection from the dead! The writer commends all of these for their great faith.

He then draws our attention to another group of believers, who also had great faith. These were tortured, scourged, chained, imprisoned, starved, driven out of their homes into the caves and open pits of the earth, went without clothing, food or shelter, were sawed in half, stoned and stabbed to death with knives and swords. The writer then commends these as well for their faith, but asserts that neither the victorious ones nor the persecuted ones received what they had been promised by God. "Only together with us, would they be made perfect" (Heb. 11:39-40). This great cloud of witnesses is waiting for our generation to finish our race; only then, will they receive what they have been promised!

As the Lord and I honestly confronted my stumbling block concerning the distinct "lack of rescue" I had experienced, as well as the murder, rape and torture of countless believers throughout time and geography, He began to teach me about the coming suffering and the falling away of His people.

This conversation caused me much pain and many tears, but the Lord was insistent that I become prepared to trust in His goodness no matter what might happen to me, or anyone else. I now record portions of that life-altering conversation. Referring to my dream and the lack of rescue, I asked the Lord what had I done wrong; He answered:

"You were a victim. You did not do anything to cause it or deserve it. Sometimes righteous people are victims."

"Are You saying that sometimes even calling on Your name will not rescue us from the situation?"

"Yes, sometimes I will not answer in the form of rescuing you. It will not be what you wanted Me to do. I do this for My own purposes in your life. Sometimes I will rescue My children, and they should always call on My name, as you did repeatedly. That was good and right, but I allowed this to take place so you will understand how it feels to be a victim, and not blame yourself for something over which you had no control.

"My children will be victims of lawlessness in these last days. Brutal and selfish

men will do worse to My children than what this man did to you. This is already happening to Christians in other countries, as you have read in the e-mails.

"*Do not be surprised and do not be angry at Me when it happens. My people will be victimized. Sometimes I will sovereignly and miraculously drive off their at-tackers. Sometimes I will not. I AM still a good God, even when men are evil.*

"*You will need to comfort My children who are victims, and you need to know it was not their fault. You will love them more because of this and will not question My goodness. [The Lord then named a brutal scenario which is occurring to some of His children now.] This can and does happen, and I AM still a good God and I love My children. Is this hard to believe?*"

"Yes," I said. "I wish You would stop these acts of violence and protect Your own ones."

"*Sometimes I do protect My own ones. Sometimes I allow My servants to suffer. I do not love them any less because I allow them to suffer at the hands of evil men. The protected ones are not loved any more than the victims. Do I love My martyrs less than the ones I keep alive until the Rapture? Surely you do not believe that!*"

I attempted not to start crying and answered, "It feels that way to my emo-tions, I must admit. I believe what You are telling me, but in my heart it feels like You love less the ones whom you allow to be beaten, raped, tortured and killed. Forgive me, Lord, but it feels that way."

At this point, I could not stop the tears, and wept bitterly. I was unable to grasp that He could love the victim just as much, and yet not stop the cruelty. I added, "My heart can't take it."

"*If you do not fully grasp My love and goodness, even when I allow you and those you love to suffer and be victims, your faith will not survive the cruelty of the lawlessness and invasion that is coming. I AM good when men are evil. I AM good when men behave well. I do not change, but men hurt My children. It has been from the beginning, since I allowed Cain to bludgeon Abel to death with an iron plow. I loved Abel more and he was the victim.[19]*

"*My people do not know what was done to My prophets or my saints, and what is being done right now to some of My most beloved sons and daughters on the earth.*

"*Are you better than My other children in other cruel places and in other cruel centuries? Is My American church so much better than all of these other people who suffered and suffer daily for My name and testimony?*

"*Why am I a good God when it happens to someone else, but a mean God when it happens to you or your loved one? My church in America needs to get real! This will happen to ALL of My Bride wherever and whenever she dwells on the face of the earth. She will be hated and will share in the fellowship of My suffering.*

[Here He reminded me of Matthew 24.]

"I love you, Jill, and I will keep you. No matter what happens to you, I love you and will keep you. Keep fighting and resisting and rejecting and rebuking the evil one. Keep calling on My name, and above all, keep trusting in My goodness when lawlessness increases and much harm comes to My most beloved ones."

This conversation continued the following day, on September 11, 2006. I was crying, as I thought of the victims of 9/11 and about our previous talk about all victims.

The Lord Jesus asked me, *"Does your heart still hurt from yesterday?"*

In response, I cried because I felt so sad that some of His children are allowed to be harmed so terribly, but He loves them just as much as the ones He protects supernaturally.

The Lord said, *"My heart hurts, too. I cry when My children suffer; don't you think I cry? Is My heart harder than yours?"*

"No, Lord, You have a tender heart; of course You cry." However, I was thinking, "You are the only one in the world big enough to stop it, and yet even though it hurts Your heart, You allow it." He knew my thoughts, of course, and we both sat in silence as the pain raged within me for awhile. It is unlikely that I will understand why He allows these things until I see Him face to face, outside of this earth's limited perspective.

The Lord then asked me if I wanted Him to heal my heart. I gladly agreed, and He instructed me to dry all of my tears, take one sip of coffee, and wait on Him. I was hoping for that most desired "anesthesia" which I have described in this chapter, but I did not feel it. He knew my thoughts and replied, *"I AM not covering your pain, as with a drug. I AM taking it away."*

Despite not receiving the desired manifestation, I knew that He was working on me, very deeply. After a period of time had elapsed, Yeshua asked me if my heart felt better.

"I feel at peace. Thank You, Healing One." I placed my hands over my heart and said, "Neither any demon nor any lawless man, nor any kind of evil thing done against me or my loved ones, can separate me from the love of Messiah. I ask You to keep the enemy far from us, but if not, I will not impugn Your character or judge Your goodness by my standards" (Dan. 3:17-18).

After this lengthy struggle, which had begun with the unthinkable dream several days before, I looked up at Him, peaceful, and with the heart and countenance of a submitted servant.

He said, *"I love you, daughter."*

I felt a wave of His love flooding me at these most treasured words, and I replied, "I love You, Ancient One."

For I am convinced that neither death nor life, neither angels nor demons, neither

*the present nor the future, nor any powers, neither height nor depth, nor anything
else in all creation, will be able to separate us from the love of God that is in Christ
Jesus* [Messiah Yeshua] *our Lord* (Rom. 8:38-39).

I believe that the reason the Lord has directed me to share this testimony as
the last one I record in this revelatory chapter, is because many of His children
will turn away from Him when these dreadful events occur.

For some reason, American Christians rarely shake their fists at God when
they read a biblical account of the brutal murder or torture of a prophet or
saint, or even the testimonies found in *Foxe's Book of Martyrs.* Some Christians,
when reading about the persecution taking place today in other countries,
might question God's goodness out of profound sympathy for the victims with
whom they might identify. (I am not suggesting that it is righteous to question
God's goodness; I am merely suggesting that it is better to feel empathy than indifference.)

Generally, however, as long as we remain safe and secure, what happens to
other people can somehow be explained away. Perhaps they did not trust Him
as much as we do. Perhaps they did not call upon the name of Jesus, or plead
His blood. Perhaps they did not rebuke the demon. Perhaps they should not
have been in that place at that time of night. Perhaps they provoked their at-
tackers needlessly, or preached a sermon which offended the government.
Perhaps they had sin in their lives and were not under His divine protection.
Perhaps they lived in a wicked city which deserved judgment, and they should
have moved away while they could. Perhaps they did not have the good fortune
to be born in America, which is blessed and protected. I myself have had some
of these thoughts on occasion, although I have also had compassionate motivations.

In His kindness to me, the Lord gave me a dream in which I was not rescued, as I fully expected to be. I questioned His goodness when He did not deliver me from my attacker. He showed me that many believers will fall away
when lawlessness increases, and the love of most will grow cold.

When formerly sheltered Christians begin to experience what is normative
for Christians in the rest of the world, and what has been suffered in all other
generations, they will impugn God's goodness and will withdraw the shallow
trust they once had placed in Him. They will believe that He does not love
them, for if He did, He would not have allowed these heinous injustices to take
place.

The Lord had to speak to me at great length and with much patience to get
me to understand that He does not love the victims less than the ones who are
miraculously protected. He does not love those whom He keeps alive more than

those whom He hands over to martyrdom or persecution.

He does not love American Christians more than any other of His sons and daughters across the globe. We are no better, and will suffer similarly. He urgently desires that His people be warned, so that when these things happen on our soil, we will not accuse Him of wrongdoing or of not loving us. Our trust in His goodness and love for each other must not grow cold, or we will be disqualified as overcomers. "He who stands firm to the end will be saved."

I pray that this difficult word will produce a harvest of love and preparation, so that we will always trust in His unfailing love no matter what harm comes to us on this earth. Whether or not we are kept safe and well on this earth is not the most critical factor; rather, we must concern ourselves with the reward of eternal life, where sorrow and pain will be forever removed.

He who has an ear, let him hear what the Spirit says to the churches. He who overcomes will not be hurt at all by the second death (Rev. 2:11).

PART III

ONE NEW MAN
IN MESSIAH

CHAPTER 9

COVENANT FRIENDSHIP

I believe that the Lord would like His people to understand the nature of a most extraordinary type of friendship called covenant friendship. This is a biblical principle, as we will fully explore in this chapter, and it has been grossly misunderstood by people who do not know the Scriptural precedents.

Some of the clearest biblical cases of covenant friendship are Ruth and Naomi, David and Jonathan, Elijah and Elisha, and Paul and Timothy. As can be seen immediately, this type of relationship is only meant to exist between two women or two men. The only covenant relationship between a man and a woman which is ordained by God is marriage. Therefore, while a Christian man and woman who are not married to each other can certainly enjoy a friendship, it must not cross the God-given boundary, or it will lead to a sinful relationship.

The predominant characteristic of this relationship is that the two friends are put together by God for His holy purposes, and not by human desire or effort. Both parties need to agree to it by their own free will, but the connection is breathed by God Himself.

Since God has put the two together, it contains some elements similar to marriage, but it is different from marriage in the following respect: in marriage, the two become one flesh (Gen. 2:24). In covenant friendship, the two always remain two separate identities; however, their prayers and worship go up to God, and He consumes this unified spiritual sacrifice as one offering. As an example, the Scriptures tell us: "Jonathan became one in spirit with David, and he loved him as he loved himself" (1 Sam. 18:1). They were one in spirit, but never "one flesh."

Due to the exceptional affection and intimacy which exists between two covenant friends, it would be easy for the world or the church to misunderstand the closeness and judge the friends as having an unclean relationship. While biblically healthy boundaries must always be guarded, it is slanderous to wrongly accuse the Lord's children, whom He has put together as holy vessels of love. In using the word "love," I am referring to godly affection, rather than a sexually intimate relationship, which the Bible states is reserved for marriage between a man and a woman.

Even so, every good gift from God can be twisted by the enemy or by the deceptiveness of sin. After we have fully explored the biblical basis for such holy partnerships, I will return to the potential dangers in such relationships, and will clearly identify the safe boundaries of purity as well as the sin which could deceive any of us.

Ruth and Naomi

Most readers are familiar with this amazing piece of Israel's history. In the days of the Judges, Elimelech and Naomi were Bethlehemites who moved to Moab due to famine in Israel. Their two sons married Moabite girls, Ruth and Orpah. Over time, Elimelech and his two sons died in this foreign land and when the famine was over, Naomi made plans to return to Israel, a bitter and desolate woman.

Naomi realizes that she is not able to bear more sons who could later marry her widowed daughters-in-law, and she urges them to return to their original families in Moab. Orpah reluctantly leaves her mother-in-law and returns to her home. Ruth, against all human logic, expresses the fiercest and most determined loyalty to Naomi, arguably among the greatest expressions ever found in the history of friendship. Ruth makes the following statement of covenant:

Don't urge me to leave you or to turn back from you. Where you go I will go, and where you stay, I will stay. Your people will be my people and your God will be my God. Where you die I will die, and there I will be buried. May the LORD deal with me, be it ever so severely, if anything but death separates you and me (Ruth 1:16-17).

The two women return to Bethlehem, and Ruth supports Naomi by gleaning food from the grain fields. Through rigorous labor in the hot sun, Ruth demonstrates unfailing love and loyalty to Naomi.

The owner of the field in which the Lord has led Ruth to glean is Boaz, a descendant of Judah and a near relative of Elimelech. He is drawn to Ruth's unusual covenant fidelity to her Israeli mother, and he begins to shower her with generous gifts of food which Ruth continually brings back with joy to Naomi.

Naomi realizes that Boaz's relationship to her late husband makes him a legal candidate to marry Ruth, according to the Law of Moses, as the "kinsman redeemer" (Deut. 25:5-10; Lev. 25:25-28). Incredibly, it is not Naomi who can alert Boaz to his Mosaic responsibility; rather, Naomi sends Ruth the Moabitess with instructions concerning Boaz and the Torah's obligations.

Since Ruth has already pledged, "Your God shall be my God," she is worthy to bring this matter before Boaz, citing the Law of Moses to him as she was taught by her Israeli mother. She also makes it clear that she loves him, which brings the proposal into a sweeter place than mere legal obligations.

The marriage which follows brings joy and restoration to Naomi's shattered hopes for a Judaic genealogy and results in the birth of David, son of Jesse; this, in turn, connects Ruth and Boaz's child to Yeshua the Messiah, the son of David and the son of God.

The elements of covenant friendship expressed in this story are unparalleled loyalty, sacrificial love and linked destinies. These friends lived and died together, praised and worshiped the God of Israel together, and produced the exalted lineage of the Davidic throne and Yeshua the Messiah together. Together, they participated in God's sovereign purposes through holy friendship.

David and Jonathan

Out of the sheepfolds of Bethlehem, God raised up a young warrior worshiper who would become Israel's most beloved and favored king, military leader and psalmist. While David was still a lad tending his father's flocks, God appointed a king to rule over Israel out of Benjamin; He did so in response to the Israeli demand for a human king, although this was not God's heart to do so. One of Saul's sons was Jonathan, a fearless soldier and a devout worshiper of the Lord (1 Sam. 14:6-14).

Against all odds, David was helped by the Lord to kill the Philistine giant, and he is brought before King Saul, where he meets Jonathan.

After David had finished talking with Saul, Jonathan became one in spirit with David, and he loved him as himself. And Jonathan made a covenant with David because he loved him as himself (1 Sam. 18:1,3).

As David grew more successful in his military campaigns to save Israel, Saul became jealous and sought to kill this brave and worthy soldier. Jonathan interceded for him and convinced Saul that David was innocent.

But David won more military acclaim and Saul, possessed by an evil spirit of hatred and jealousy, attempted to murder him while the loyal psalmist was playing the harp for the king. Saul then sent men to David's home to kill him, and he became a hunted man from that point on. Finally, David sought help from Jonathan; perhaps his covenant friend could intercede again for David with his demonized father, the king. David explained the situation, and Jonathan pledged to help him. The two friends agreed on a plan to test Saul's intentions. Before they implemented the plan, Jonathan and David reaffirmed their covenant of friendship.

In the end, Jonathan sadly realized that his father did indeed plan to

murder David. They met one last time in the field where they had set up the secret signals. They kissed and wept and parted forever on this earth (1 Sam. 18:5-
20:42).

There are some who would wish to portray the relationship of David and
Jonathan as a sexual relationship; there is no scriptural evidence for this asser-
tion, and I believe that to attach this perspective to their godly friendship does
an injustice to the biblical account and to their memories.

The primary verse which some have cited as evidence for a sexual element
in their friendship is a lament composed by David after Jonathan was killed
with his father in battle. One line in this lyrical composition is:

> *I grieve for you, Jonathan my brother; you were very dear to me. Your love for me*
> *was wonderful, more wonderful than that of women* (2 Sam. 1:26).

To analyze this declaration of David's love, it is important to look at his relationship with the women he loved as well. Despite David's exalted status in
Scripture as "a man after God's own heart," he still had character flaws, as does
every man and woman. Genesis records that God's original intention was for
one man and one woman to marry; this principle is taught and emphasized by
our Lord Yeshua as well (Matt. 19:4-9; Gen. 1:27). David took many wives and
concubines, as did some other Old Testament figures. Solomon's polygamy, particularly with hundreds of foreign women, turned his heart away from the one
true God and caused him to build high places for idolatrous worship.

Since the Scripture says that a man and a woman shall become "one flesh,"
how can this union occur when the husband has multiple wives and concubines? Is the man "one flesh" with all of them? Are all the women, therefore,
"one flesh" with each other? This God-ordained union is not actually possible in
cases of polygamy.

Jacob was tricked into marrying Leah before he was granted Rachel; but
even in this case of only two wives, Jacob could only love one of them. He im-
pregnated Leah many times, but his heart always belonged to Rachel until the
day she died. The jealousy and ugly rivalry between the two sisters was a tragic
condition brought about by Laban's treachery. Polygamy violates God's creation
and the standards He intended for marriage. The Apostle Paul writes to
Timothy that any man in church leadership must be the husband of only one
wife; clearly Paul does not permit a godly man to commit polygamy (1 Tim.
3:1-4).

Therefore, I believe that David could not have found the deep, one-on-one
intimacy with his many women that he was able to find in the emotionally satisfying friendship he had with Jonathan. It is very possible that some of David's

wives and concubines rarely even saw him, let alone enjoying intimate conversations with him. Some of these women may have only encountered him on one night; they were then physically cared for in the harem but emotionally neglected from that point on. Once a king had been intimate with a girl, no other man could ever have her, on pain of treason and death (1 Kings 2:13-25). Therefore, she was forever in the king's harem, whether or not he ever called for her again. (We see this in the book of Esther, as well.)

This lament of David expresses an intimate and enduring friendship, in which the love he shared with Jonathan exceeded the love David was able to share with his numerous wives and concubines. I believe David was able to share confidences with Jonathan that he would not confide in one of his wives. They were able to worship the Lord together in songs and in prayer on a level that David may not have experienced with his wives. They also risked their lives as Israeli soldiers together, which creates a tremendous bond of brotherhood. Therefore, it is my conclusion that this verse is not a reference to physical intimacy; rather, it is an expression of emotional intimacy. They were brothers, not in the flesh but in the spirit.

After Jonathan and Saul's deaths, David sought to fulfill his promise to bless Jonathan's remaining family; this is quite remarkable, considering what Saul had done to David. It would be expected that once David came into his seat of authority, he would destroy the house of Saul. However, not only did David not seek revenge on Saul's children, but he actually put to death those who murdered Saul's son Ish-Bosheth, thinking they were doing David a favor (2 Sam. 4:9). Later, David was required to hand over seven of Saul's descendants to the Gibeonites, but he spared Mephibosheth, who was the crippled son of Jonathan (2 Sam. 21:7). This affirms the verse which says:

> *Place me like a seal over your heart, like a seal on your arm; For love is as strong as death, its jealousy unyielding as the grave. It burns like blazing fire, like a mighty flame. May waters cannot quench love; rivers cannot wash it away* (Song of Songs 8:6-7).

This covenant friendship between two devout young Israeli soldiers was put together by the God of Israel. The Lord used this relationship to expose Saul's wickedness and to preserve David's life until he could become the God-ordained King of Israel. Through this royal position of authority, David would achieve significant victories over Israel's enemies and take back much of the Promised Land which had been given on oath by the Lord Almighty to Abraham.

In addition, David's position as King would lead to the births of Solomon and Nathan; both of these Davidic sons are found in the royal lineage of Jesus the Messiah, as recorded by Matthew and Luke. Solomon's line produced Miriam (Mary), our Lord's mother; Nathan's line produced Joseph, the Lord's legal and ancestral father, though not His biological parent. Thus the holy friendship between David and Jonathan was birthed by the Lord for His own covenant purposes.

Paul and Timothy

In a brief overview of this intense and trusting friendship, Paul indicates in his letters that at the end, the only friend Paul could truly count on was his "son" Timothy. Paul met this young disciple in Lystra after a painful disagreement with Barnabus and a parting of ways (Acts 15). Paul and Timothy quickly became close, and Paul decided to take him along on his next ministry trip. He circumcised Timothy, as a Jewish father would do for his own son; Timothy's father was Greek, and despite his Jewish mother, he had not been circumcised on the eighth day after his birth. Paul had no physical children, and his heart was drawn toward this God-given spiritual son.

To the Corinthians, Paul writes, "I am sending to you Timothy, my son, whom I love, who is faithful in the Lord" (1 Cor. 4:17). To the Philippians, he writes, "I have no one else like him…Timothy has proved himself, because as a son with his father, he has served me in the work of the gospel" (Php. 2:20-22). In Paul's second letter to Timothy, he writes, "Recalling your tears, I long to see you, so that I may be filled with joy." He also writes that everyone else has deserted him, and he can only count on this friend to remain faithful.

I believe that this was more than an ordinary friendship. It seems from the Scriptural accounts that Paul and Timothy were covenant friends; this was a holy partnership breathed by the Lord for the spreading of the Gospel, the writing of epistles and the establishment of churches.

This relationship aided Paul in the difficult and discouraging work of bringing the Gospel to the Gentile nations, while enduring fierce opposition from his own people and severe physical hardships. Without this support and comfort, his infirmities and woundings, imprisonment and mental anguish might have hindered the costly assignment which our Lord had given him: "I will make you a light to the Gentiles, that you may bring Yeshua (salvation) to the ends of the earth" (Php. 2:28; 2 Cor. 11:24-28; Acts 13:47).

My Covenant Friendship

I have enjoyed a number of friendships over the years, but only a few were very close and enduring. Even so, none of these could rightly be called "covenant friendships." They lacked the spiritual unity of purpose and the holy attributes required to meet this high, heavenly standard of friendship. In recent years, the Lord has surprised me with a unique friendship with a woman who appears a number of times in this book of my testimony; her name is Katya.

We did not seek to become friends, nor did we have much in common. Our personalities were quite diverse, and we did not have any instant connection when we first met. For quite a while, the primary activities which Katya and I shared were intercession, worship and planning regional spiritual gatherings. It was in this context that we began to realize the Lord was doing something unusual with us.

It began one day when Katya came into the church office where I worked and shared that the Lord had put an exact date on her heart for a special prayer and worship meeting. She shared a general sense of what the meeting should contain. I had a suspicion, but quickly checked my calendar just to be sure: the date she had received was the biblical Feast of Trumpets, and the activities she proposed were in keeping with a holiday she knew almost nothing about! Katya, as a non-Jewish believer, had never known or followed the biblical feasts, nor was she aware of their dates and seasons. I was impressed, and we worked together on this meeting which was greatly blessed that year.

In the spring she approached me with a word she received about a particular date, again specifying an unusual act of repentance and intercession. Interestingly, it turned out to be the Day of Preparation for Passover and was the day on which the Jewish people cleanse their homes from leaven and prepare for the seven days of the Feast of Unleavened Bread.

Late in the summer this synergy happened again, this time with a more obscure Jewish holiday which even most Jews do not observe: the ninth of Av, a day of mourning over the destruction of the Temple in Jerusalem. Katya was not aware of this day on the calendar, and yet she was very insistent that the intercessors fast and blow the shofar towards Jerusalem at sunset on the eve of this solemn day.

Both of us realized that she was hearing from the Holy Spirit, and I was providing the biblical and historical connection to the dates and activities she was receiving. The fourth example of this partnership pertained to the ceremonial pouring out of water on the Feast of Tabernacles. Again, I was able to supply the teaching and Scriptural background for what she was hearing from the Lord's Spirit. We began to realize that God had put us together as a symbolic picture of the "marriage" between the Word and the Spirit. I was a teacher of the Word and of the biblical calendar; Katya heard very accurately from the Holy Spirit.

The partnership grew steadily from this point. It would fill another book if I were to document the dozens of astonishing words, confirmations, strategies, dreams, ministry connections and purposes which the Lord birthed through our holy partnership.

As we spoke on the phone or in person, we did not discuss the everyday topics as normal friends would do. Of course I am not suggesting that normal conversations between friends are wrong; I am only making a distinction between a normal Christian friendship with which the Lord is pleased, and the set-apart relationships which He has ordained for His Kingdom purposes. When we spoke, Katya and I would only discuss matters of spiritual significance which the Lord was showing us; in numerous cases, He would give me a piece of the puzzle and would supply Katya with the complementary piece, so that only when conferring together would the full revelation become clear. When she and I prayed together, the presence of the Lord began to come strongly, and our special love for each other grew gradually over a three-year period.

Katya began to accompany me, as well as several other precious intercessors, to strategic intercessory conferences. She also prayed fervently for me as I taught in various churches and meetings; I was quite aware that her prayer covering was an essential part of the gracious anointing which the Lord had poured upon my teachings.

Acceleration!

It is hard to describe what happened next. It seemed that time was accelerating at a breathless pace, and strategies, plans and fulfillments were occurring so quickly that we could not even keep up with them or with each other. If three days elapsed between phone calls, we could never find enough time to share what the Lord had shown us or done in our hearts over those last days. My journal entries began to grow exponentially, and I could not write often enough or fast enough to record the staggering flow of spiritual events. Even in the writing of this book, so much has happened since I began writing thirty-four days ago, that I am adding new material daily and find it difficult to know when to "cut if off" for the sake of ending a chapter.

This rapid acceleration is a signpost of living in the last days. Evidence of this phenomenon includes: disasters, inventions, pharmaceutical advances, technological changes, evangelization of the third world, nuclear threats and rumors of war, terrorist activities, political agitation and enmities, the increase in healings and miracles, prophetic strategies and the simultaneous growth of both the "wheat" and the "tares" (Matt. 13:24-43). Surely, just as Elijah ran to Jezreel with supernatural speed ahead of Ahab's chariot before the heavy rains fell, this is the season to run at maximum speed and to keep up with the pace of the Spirit's accelerated activities upon the earth in the days preceding His judgments and His return.

Linked Destinies

In the fall of 2005 while at the conference in Birmingham, Katya received a difficult word from the Lord Jesus. She was not permitted to tell me about it until the next day. It was shocking to me, and frankly, I only partially believed it at the time. During a quiet period of worship and waiting, the Lord told her that her hands and feet would be pierced and that she would give her life for Him. She thought He might be referring to His own hands and feet, but He made it clear that He was speaking about her future and not His past. At the time, I had not yet experienced my three days and knew nothing of my own future martyrdom. I received her word quietly and sadly but couldn't imagine a scenario in which this kind of piercing would take place. After all, crucifixion is not the preferred method of execution in any nation that I'm aware of.

In May of the following year, Katya took three days to be apart with the Lord, just as I had done in April. During this time, the Lord showed her much more detail about her future ministry, location, and martyrdom. She too was called to a nation in Europe, but it was not the same nation that He had shown me. The Lord gave Katya a supernatural sign involving a physical nail to confirm that He was indeed speaking to her about this matter.

When her three days were ended, Katya came to my house and spent several hours reading to me from her journal. As she shared the portion concerning her death, I began to grieve deeply. Several elements were excessively hard to bear: we would be geographically separated for a significant amount of time in our respective countries, doing the work our Lord had prepared for us, and she would die shortly before I was to die. I did not want to outlive my precious friend and was dismayed by this news. Katya shared that when I would hear the report of her death, I would be greatly strengthened and encouraged to face my own death, which would come very soon after her own.

The Lord also made her an astonishing offer, which some readers might find difficult to believe: He asked her if she would like to wait for me to complete my race before her spirit went up to Him. Katya answered that she would like that very much, and the Lord Yeshua showed her the scenario in which her spirit, as well as two angels and two saints, would stand by to accompany my spirit when it was set free from my body through martyrdom. I would not be able to see them until the very end, as I departed.

This revelation caused me a depth of grief I have never known. Katya is the most gentle and generous person I have ever met, and the thought of cruel and merciless men harming her was too much for me. The reality of this destiny and the linkage between our lives and deaths completely overwhelmed me, and I began to weep so hard and for so long, it seemed I would never finish. Over the next few hours, the sadness swallowed me up. I lay upon Katya's shoulder and sobbed, and I didn't want her to go home. I wanted to kiss her hands and keep her safe and close, but knew that I could not. I found myself intensely needing to be held and comforted, which is extremely unusual for me.

After she went home, I went upstairs to be with the Lord. At first, I flopped on the bed and contemplated curling up in a ball and wallowing in the inconsolable anguish of my soul. However, I decided that was not what my Lord would want me to do, and so I made a choice to get up, dry my eyes, and play my guitar for Him. Then I sat in my rocking chair to talk to Him honestly about my pain. That turned out to be a very good decision indeed.

I had prayed and then placed my tallit over my head; with uncovered face and eyes open, I began to talk to the Lord about the force of this grief. I talked for about five or ten minutes and then began to feel my eyelids getting heavy and my speech becoming difficult and unclear. I wondered, "Could I be falling asleep?" I knew this was highly unlikely, since I can barely sleep at night, let alone in the middle of the day. I tried to tell the Lord I felt sleepy. I said, "I feel...I feel..." I was not able to finish this sentence because a heavy sweet presence enveloped me, my speech became impossible, and my eyes could not remain open. I now understood that this was not about sleep, and my last thought was, "Oh, I know what this is!"

The Lord's peace and restfulness covered my mind, body and spirit, and there was suddenly no room for grief. I stayed in this state for about twenty minutes, and it finally faded away. All of my pain was gone and has never returned! I rested in bed to recover, and Katya called to see if I was alright. I told her that He healed my heart in His glory because I waited on Him; I had talked to Him openly about my great pain instead of privately indulging in despair. I thanked the Lord Yeshua for His mercy to me. Because I chose not to suffer apart from Him but rather came to Him directly, He rewarded me and took away my despair. The most important element of this true story is the need for complete transparency before the Lord, at the moment of our deepest grief. We must never shut Him out of our sorrow or suffer apart from Him; this would hurt the Lord deeply.

The Spirit of the Sovereign LORD is on me...to comfort all who mourn and provide for those who grieve in Zion; to bestow on them a crown of beauty instead of ashes, the oil of gladness instead of mourning, and a garment of praise instead of a spirit of despair (Isa. 61:1-3).

One New Man in Messiah

In the second chapter of Ephesians, Paul explains a wondrous mystery. This promise has been throbbing in the heart of the Father since He spoke the following words to Abraham, fresh and living words that radiate down through the ages into our destinies:

I will make you into a great nation and I will bless you. I will make your name great, and you will be a blessing. I will bless those who bless you, and whoever curses you I will curse; and all peoples on earth will be blessed through you (Gen. 12:2-3).

It was always the Lord's intention to gather to Himself a bride from among the nations. He made an irrevocable covenant with Abraham and his descendents; this would become the means by which He would include all nations in His Messianic redemptive plan.

The Messianic promise was first to Abraham's physical seed, through the lineage of Isaac and Jacob; in the fullness of time, this chosen genealogy would give birth to Yeshua of Nazareth, the Son of David and the Son of the Living God (Gen. 17:19-21; Gal. 4:4).

Through Abraham's descendent, the Lord Yeshua, God-fearing people from all nations can be included in the blessings and promises given to our beloved patriarch. This is because the Messiah's offspring consist of a vast company of spiritual children from all nations, who have trusted in His atonement and His faithfulness, as did Abraham (Rom. 4:16; Gal. 3:14). By trusting in God and being faithful to Him, these "children" are behaving like their spiritual father, Abraham, who was still uncircumcised and had not yet become a "Hebrew" at the time he trusted in God's promise to him (Rom. 4:9-12).

In the Hebrew language, a "son of" someone or something is not always about physical descent; rather, it is a descriptive title conveying that the "son" reflects the behavioral attributes of his "father." For example, a "son of light" displays the qualities of light; a "son of perdition" exhibits the characteristics of being lost and doomed; the "sons of thunder" were volatile and commanded attention; a "son of encouragement," as Barnabus was called, is motivated to encourage others. (These four examples are found in John 12:36, 17:12; Mk. 3:17, Acts 4:36).

In the same way, a "son of Abraham" will display the attributes of Abraham: obedience, faith in God and trust in His promises against all odds. This is the background from which Paul understood that physical lineage was not as important as behavior, in determining who is a "son of Abraham" and who is not.

The Lord Yeshua affirmed this Hebraic understanding of who is called a "son of Abraham" in His discussion with Jewish people "who had believed Him" (John 8:31). It is strange to me that the passage says that they believed Him and yet somehow, they were still so threatened by Him that they were determined to kill Him. Did they only believe Him with their minds but not love Him in their hearts? It would seem so, for Yeshua tells them that to claim "sonship" of Abraham, one must display the behavior and attributes of Abraham. A person is a "son of" the person or idea whose behavior he imitates!

Jesus said, "If you were Abraham's children, then you would do the things Abraham did. As it is, you are determined to kill me, a man who has told you the truth that I heard from God. Abraham did not do such things. You are doing the things your own father does" (John 8:39-41).

This is a very Hebraic mindset and reminds us that the Lord said, "Be perfect, therefore, as your heavenly Father is perfect" (Matt. 5:48). If the Father is perfect, His sons and daughters are to reflect that perfection!

Paul, the renowned Judaic scholar, was assigned by the Lord to be an apostle to the Gentiles, and he had a great love for the spiritual "sons of Abraham." Paul understood God's heartfelt desire to graft the nations into His covenant of salvation through the Jewish Messiah Yeshua (Rom 11:17-18). As he addressed the Ephesians, he laid the foundation for the mystery revealed in Chapter 3:

Therefore, remember that formerly you who are gentiles by birth…remember that at that time you were separated from Christ, excluded from citizenship in Israel and foreigners to the covenants of the promise, without hope and without God in the world. But now in Christ Jesus [Messiah Yeshua] you who once were far away have been brought near through the blood of Christ. His purpose was to create in Himself One New Man out of the two, thus making peace, and in this one body to reconcile both of them to God through the cross, by which He put to death their hostility (Eph. 2:11-16).

Paul continues in the next chapter with the unveiling of the "mystery of Messiah," formerly hidden, but now "made real to me through revelation" (Eph. 3:3).

This mystery is that through the gospel the gentiles are heirs together with Israel, members together of one body, and sharers together in the promise in Christ Jesus [Messiah Yeshua] (Eph. 3:6).

Just as there are covenant friendships between individuals, God has purposed to create a corporate "covenant friendship" between Jewish and Gentile believers! It is the Lord's intention that there would be rich and loving fellowship, worship, intercession and the gifts of the Holy Spirit, flowing freely between Jewish and Gentile worshipers.

Therefore, it is extremely significant that my covenant friendship with Katya is a Jewish/Gentile friendship. We have both sensed that this is extremely precious to Him, and He has magnified the effects of the partnership to a higher level than what either of us could have attained individually. Of course, this principle is true in a general sense; each member of the Lord's body needs each other, in order that the whole body may be complete. Nevertheless, I am stunned at the multiplication which has resulted from our holy partnership, and I have no doubt that He is raising up similar partnerships among His own ones in every part of the earth where His people dwell. The covenant friendship which is of the highest order is the one He creates now, even today: the One New Man in Messiah.

The Misuse of Covenant Friendship

An immature or emotionally unstable believer can enter into a relationship which may begin as a godly friendship; however, it can become unhealthy if it enters the realm of codependency or even sexuality. God did not ordain covenant friendship to include either of these elements, and both situations constitute an abuse of the pure friendship the Lord desired. This abuse can take several forms, depending on the weaknesses and woundedness of the individuals involved.

One misuse of covenant friendship is when a man and woman cross the boundary of ordinary friendship into covenant friendship, which is only meant to be exercised and released within marriage. Crossing this boundary will often result in emotional or physical adultery.

For Christians to enjoy healthy male/female friendships, clear boundaries must always be observed. These include issues of physical touch, emotional intimacy, and not keeping secrets from each friend's spouse. Any mature counselor or pastor can advise people on these matters.

I would suspect that most believers have at some time, observed or participated in the crossing of biblical boundaries between male and female friends. I myself crossed into this unhealthy territory when I entered the secret world of emotional attachment to a man who was not my husband, as recounted in Chapter 2.

A second misuse of covenant friendship is when the relationship moves into the area of sensuality between two friends of the same sex. The guidelines for these friendships are similar to the guidelines between men and women who are not married to each other. The Scriptures are explicit about all forms of sexual sin, and no amount of philosophical or political acrobatics can change this fact. Sometimes a friendship can move into this arena before the friends are fully aware of it. Sensual behavior can develop due to the influence of seducing spirits, or due to certain emotional weaknesses or tendencies in one or both of the friends.

Let me state clearly that our gentle and gracious Lord loves all those He created, knowing that we are all sinful and fall short of His holy standards. While His righteousness will not allow Him to excuse or condone sinful behavior, the Lord Jesus offers freedom and forgiveness to any person who acknowledges their sin and wishes to be free of any temptation or sinful lifestyle. He loves all sinners, and all are welcome to accept His offer of salvation and freedom from the yoke of sin. Whoever will ask for mercy will receive it freely through His blood atonement because "mercy triumphs over judgment" (James 2:13).

Even so, the Lord will not be mocked in His righteous standards for human behavior. His laws and precepts are immutable, and lawlessness (those who deliberately and continually live outside of God's Law) will give an account to God, even if it has to wait until the last day.

The Lord's Help and Mercy Are Available

In the following true story, the names have been changed for obvious reasons. A number of years ago I was counseling a young woman named Crystal, barely twenty-one years old at the time. She was raised by Christian parents and attended church all of her life. After moving out, she began attending another church and became very close friends with Carli, who was in her thirties. Carli was raised in this church, and her parents were elders for many years; Carli also had a ministry within church leadership.

Crystal and Carli were inseparable; they talked constantly on the phone, including all hours of the night. They attended church activities together and joined the young singles group. I truly don't know if the Lord intended this to be a covenant friendship or just a normal friendship. When I would ask if they prayed together, I always got a vague answer.

After several years of close friendship, they finally planned a trip together. They booked a room and drove to a desert resort for a one-week break. About four months after returning from vacation, Crystal called me in a state of suicidal depression. I invited her to come over and tell me what happened. She came over that night, and as she told me this story, I was appalled but not completely shocked; I sensed it was reflective of a serious problem affecting a large segment of the church, involving a wide variety of sexual sins.

In brief, Crystal told me that within the first two days of their vacation, Carli declared that she had always been in love with her and made strong sexual advances. Crystal said that she was uncomfortable but could not risk hurting or rejecting her best friend. Her fear of losing the relationship was greater than her reluctance to enter this dimension. After thinking about Carli's urgent request, she agreed, and this relationship continued for several months.

Eventually, church leadership found out about the affair and questioned each woman separately. Each blamed the other for initiating the relationship. The elders of the church required that the two women end the friendship completely. Within a few short days, what had been a longstanding, warm friendship was transformed into a cold separation, including blame, shame and hostility.

This tragic story illustrates the destruction caused by sin and the unraveling of the good plans and purposes of the Lord for His children. He may well have put these two bright and sensitive women together for the purpose of growth, prayer and mutual support. They may even have been appointed to enter into a covenant friendship at some point, perhaps when they had matured in their prayer life and intimacy with the Lord.

But sin, seizing its moment, took what God intended for good and distorted it into an unhealthy and inappropriate relationship which caused harm to many lives. Of course, forgiveness and healing were fully available to both women. I believe the church treated them with kindness at the time of this incident. Whenever we sin, the Lord will readily remove our sin by His spotless blood, wash us clean, fill us with His Spirit and give us a fresh start (Psalm 51).

For anyone who may be struggling with an unwholesome relationship, whether male/female or same-sex, or a flirtation which has the potential to do great damage, there is excellent help available from a number of Christian sources.[20]

The Importance of Inner Healing

There are steps we can take to protect ourselves from an emotional vulnerability which could endanger a friendship, causing it to move into a sinful situation. It is important for every believer to receive inner healing from the Lord for past emotional wounds or physical traumas. It is also vital to receive forgiveness from the Lord for our sinful responses to those wounds. There are several excellent resources for Scriptural-based prayer counseling in which this inner healing can take place in a safe atmosphere. One of the best ministries available to Christians is "Elijah House," founded by John and Paula Sandford.[21] The following quote is an excerpt from the website, and there are many locations throughout the country where this ministry is offered. My own pastor, Sandra

Shantz, serves as a Facilitator of these in-depth courses of study, prayer and healing offered by Elijah House.

> As Christians, we tend to press on in terms of managing behavior rather than renewing our mind and receiving a new heart, which naturally changes behavior. Many have tried to forget "what lies behind" (Philippians 3:13) by ignoring the past rather than by letting the Holy Spirit search the innermost parts of the heart in order to allow Jesus to deal specifically with deeply ingrained attitudes. They have attempted to put aside the old self with its practices of anger, wrath, malice and slander, as if these were present, external expressions only, whereas Jesus called the Pharisees (and us) to "clean the *inside* of the cup" (Matthew 23:36).
>
> There are several ingredients in ministry conducted at Elijah House and imparted through our training, to facilitate the process of sanctification. All ingredients are grounded in Scripture and led of the Holy Spirit. At their center are these three, which call us to wholeness:
> • Repentance: exercising godly grief based on love for God and for those who have been wounded, resulting in real change.
> • Confession: bringing what has been held in secret to the light.
> • Forgiveness: releasing those who have hurt us to God, and asking Him to forgive us for our own sin.
>
> It is by these three acts that we are reconciled to God and to one another. Christ's work is complete, but God is still at work in our lives. True freedom requires first recognizing that many of today's problems have their roots in our sinful responses to yesterday's wounds and cannot easily be erased by fleshly efforts at good behavior. For more in-depth information about sanctification and transformation, read John and Paula Sandford's classic book, *Transformation of the Inner Man.*

The Innocence of Covenant Friendship

Having covered the dangers and misuses of covenant friendship, I also need to clarify the innocent expressions of friendship and physical affection which God has ordained and which are found throughout the Scriptures, between friends of the same gender.

Just as it is wrong to ignore sinful behavior, it is equally wrong to accuse upright and pure friendships of sexual elements which do not exist. In virtually every teaching epistle of Paul and Peter, we find the phrase, "Greet the brothers with a holy kiss." It is evident that ancient and modern men in the Middle East affectionately greet each other with a kiss, and it is not connected with sexual behavior.

David and Jonathan kissed each other (1Sam 20:41), Judas greeted Yeshua in the garden with a kiss, which appears to be an expected greeting (Matt 26:49), and Peter and Paul treat this gesture as a holy act of affection between believers. The disciple John laid his head upon Yeshua's breast during the Last Supper, one of the tenderest and most endearing images found in Scripture.

Let the reader consider: If you saw a man in church lay his head upon the pastor's breast and rest upon him like a contented child, would you rejoice or judge? If two female friends did this in church, would you be offended? Is it a biblically permissible gesture, or is it sin? Do we assume the best or the worst about someone's heart?

It is the corruption in our culture which causes innocent and childlike love to appear sensual or inappropriate. As exemplified in Jane Austin's novels, the purity and innocence, even prudishness, of the Victorian Era are evident. Even so, women often held hands during this era, embraced and kissed, and took public walks with their arms linked. Interestingly, during this same era, men and women were never seen exhibiting this affection in public, even those engaged to be married. Some of the higher quality film productions of Victorian novels portray these safe and sisterly gestures of love.

In our current culture, most men would not wish to display this affection with their male friends, due to insecurity about what others would think; however, it would not be sinful to do so if they were involved in a pure and brotherly friendship. King David wrote:

> *The Lord has rewarded me according to my righteousness, according to the cleanness of my hands in His sight. To the faithful you show yourself faithful, to the blameless you show yourself blameless, to the pure you show yourself pure, but to the crooked, you show yourself shrewd* (Psalm 18:24-26).

Love is Stronger than Death

When I first heard the word which the Lord Yeshua gave to Katya concerning our deaths, I was stunned that such a thing was possible, although I could see no biblical reason why it was not possible. According to her testimony, the Lord told her that her spirit, after her own martyrdom, would be permitted to wait in the earthly realm for my martyrdom and that we would be granted to ascend together to be with the Lord forever. Although I would not be able to see her, nor would there be any communication, she would be waiting for me. I wondered if anything like this had ever been mentioned in ancient texts about the connected martyrdom of two covenant friends.

Soon after this, through a dear and scholarly friend, I learned of two Christian military martyrs who suffered for their faith during the reign of the

Roman emperor Galerius Maximianus (305-11). Their names were Sergius and Bacchus, and much has been written about them due to the cult of martyr veneration common among the fourth and fifth century Christians. A brief summary of their testimony is presented here.[22]

Both men were officers in the imperial bodyguard unit of the Roman army in the Syrian province of the Roman Empire; Sergius was a senior officer. The emperor treated them with favor, and other members of this elite unit became envious. Sergius and Bacchus were then accused of being Christians and of convincing others to become Christians as well, which violated the Roman laws requiring the worship of pagan gods.

Maximianus decided to test Sergius and Bacchus to see if the informers' accusations were true. He ordered them to sacrifice at the temple of Zeus, which they refused to do. The emperor was enraged by their refusal and marched them through the town, stripped of their military uniforms, heavily chained and dressed in women's clothes for the purpose of humiliating them before the army. They were sent quite a distance to the Duke Antiochus for trial; he was a military commander who had attained his high position through Sergius' connections.

These two officers were inseparable Christian brothers in the Lord and had often sung hymns to God together before their arrest. Antiochus ordered them tortured and executed due to their refusal to worship the Greek gods. Sergius and Bacchus continued to pray, sing songs to the Lord, and ask forgiveness for the brutal men who inflicted these hideous pains upon them throughout their ordeal.

Bacchus was scourged to death over several hours. Sergius was forced to run for nine miles, ahead of Antiochus' chariot, with nails driven through the soles of his boots. In prison that night, his feet were healed by an angel. Antiochus was so angry about the healing that he forced Sergius to run another nine miles on nails. On the night after Bacchus' death, Sergius was so overwhelmed with grief at the death of his friend that he wavered in his faith and despaired of enduring. Bacchus then appeared to him, radiant and glorious, and told him of the glory that awaited him; he encouraged him to hang on so that they would be together forever. Finally, Sergius was beheaded, when no amount of torture could break his spirit. As an historical note, this horrific persecution occurred only about fifteen years before the Emperor Constantine outlawed the torture and execution of Christians.

In researching these martyrs, I was dismayed to see that a few websites declared them to be early examples of "same-sex marriage" within the Catholic Church. These cited the friends' extraordinary statements of affection and love for each other, as recorded in the texts. After research and prayer, I have come to this conclusion about Sergius and Bacchus: I believe they were covenant friends and devout young Roman soldiers, just as David and Jonathan were covenant friends and devout young Israeli soldiers. As with David and Jonathan, they were not in a sexual relationship, and I believe the Lord has confirmed this to me.

The historical evidence for my conclusion is as follows: the Roman army had no tolerance for homosexuality and had these high-ranking officers been conducting this type of affair, the punishment would have been mutilation and death. Despite the horrible tortures inflicted on them, they were not emasculated, and the charges against them were limited to the refusal to worship pagan gods. Therefore, they were killed for the cause of Messiah.

I believe that the Lord allowed Bacchus to encourage his covenant friend, and I believe He will allow Katya to wait for me to complete my testimony before our spirits ascend to the Lord. An angel from heaven was sent to strengthen our Lord in the garden as He prepared for His suffering (Luke 22:43). The Lord told us that in the resurrection, we will be like the angels.

> But those who are considered worthy of taking place in that age and in the resurrection from the dead...can no longer die, for they are like the angels. They are God's children, since they are children of the resurrection. But in the account of the bush, even Moses showed that the dead rise, for he calls the Lord "the God of Abraham, and the God of Isaac, and the God of Jacob." He is not the God of the dead, but of the living, for to him all are alive (Luke 20:35-38).

Even though the bodily resurrection of Abraham, Isaac and Jacob had not yet taken place when Yeshua spoke these words (and still has not occurred), He still considered these saints to be alive to God, "children of the resurrection."

Paul makes it clear that the physical resurrection of the bodies of the righteous dead will not take place until the Lord returns to gather His elect, both those who have died in Messiah and those who are still alive when He comes (1 Cor. 15:22-23; 1 Thess. 4:15-17). Since my passing will take place before the Rapture of the "sleeping" and living believers, the day of the physical resurrection of the dead will still be a future event. Even so, according to the Lord's word, all of those believers who have died and who will die before the Rapture are considered "children of the resurrection" and thus, "like the angels."

Those who have given their lives before us, the "great cloud of witnesses," are alive with the Lord in heaven. They are aware of events on earth and could certainly visit us briefly on assignment, if the Lord so directed, just as angels were sent to earth on assignments throughout the Bible.

The desperate King Saul wickedly consulted the witch of Endor in order to speak to the departed prophet Samuel, who had made him king; this was the sin of consulting the dead, forbidden in the Torah. Nevertheless, it was the Sovereign Lord Himself who sent the prophet Samuel back to earth to prophesy one last time over this doomed and reprobate king. The Scriptures depict very clearly that it is Samuel who speaks to Saul, and his message is the identical, righteous judgment which he spoke in the days of his life.

The Lord can initiate any interaction between heaven and earth that suits His purposes and encourages His suffering children. The Lord does not consider the cloud of witnesses to be dead but considers them to be living saints.

Place me like a seal over your heart, like a seal on your arm; For love is as strong as death, its jealousy unyielding as the grave (Song of Songs 8:6a).

CHAPTER 10

WHY DO THE NATIONS RAGE?

For the Bride of Messiah to be in intimate fellowship with her husband, the Lord Yeshua, she must know His heart for His brothers of human lineage, the Jewish people. The Lord carries unceasing grief in His heart for those of His people who do not yet know His sacrifice and salvation. The Lord has directed me to conclude this book with His unfailing love and faithfulness to His covenants with the physical descendants of Abraham, Isaac and Jacob.

The following psalm was written by Asaph three thousand years ago, and yet it seems as fresh and relevant as the summer headlines:

O God, do not keep silent; be not quiet, O God, be not still. See how your enemies are astir, how your foes rear their head With cunning they conspire against your people, they plot against those you cherish. "Come," they say, "let us destroy them as a nation, that the name of Israel be remembered no more. With one mind they plot together, they form an alliance against you... May they ever be ashamed and dismayed; may they perish in disgrace. Let them know that you, whose name is the Lord, that you alone are the Most High over all the earth" (Psalm 83:1-5,17-18).

Is it astonishing that, three thousand years later, the exact same enemy nations named in this psalm, exhibit the identical hatred and determination to destroy this tiny Jewish nation? For nineteen hundred years, this people had been driven from their land to the four corners of the earth; yet the moment the people of Israel are restored as a nation, the same ancient enemies rise up to annihilate them; doesn't this seem remarkable?

Can dry and disconnected bones in the desert come together into a living army? (Ezek. 37)

Can a withered fig tree sprout leaves and bear fruit? (Matt. 21:18-19; Matt. 24:32-33)

Can a nation be born in a day, or a country be brought forth in a moment? (Isa. 66:7-8)

Can springs gush in the desert, and flowers and orchards flourish in the wilderness? (Isa. 35)

Can the veil of blindness over a people's eyes be lifted, and vivid sight be restored? (Zech. 12:10; Rom. 11:25-27)

Can the glory of God return to Jerusalem? (Isa. 4:5-6; Ezek. 43:7; Zech. 14:4; Isa. 52:8)

The Unconditional Covenant

Out of Ur of the Chaldees, God called Abram to become the father of many nations; He made a covenant with Abram and granted to him and to his descendants a particular tract of unfamiliar land, hundreds of miles west of Chaldea (Gen. 12:1-3; Gen. 15). This passage describes the "cutting of a covenant," a common method of ratifying a treaty in the ancient Near East when a sacrifice was cut in half lengthwise, and each piece was laid on either side of a shallow gully. The blood of the animal would run down into the gully and form a pool. The ruler and his subject, who were entering into covenant, would both walk past each other through the blood. They would take an oath saying, "May this be done to me if I do not uphold my part of this treaty."

In Genesis 15, we see that God put Abram into a deep sleep; the Lord alone, in the form of a blazing torch, walked through the river of blood in the middle of the sacrifice. By this extraordinary gesture, He was signifying that He alone was responsible to keep the covenant and that Abram was not required to walk through or take an oath, as would have been expected. Since no conditions were placed on Abraham, this is called an "unconditional land grant covenant."

Although Ishmael was born earlier through Hagar, the Lord confirmed this land grant to Isaac, the promised child born in Sarah's old age (Gen. 26:3-4).

> And Abraham said to God, "If only Ishmael might live under your blessing!" Then God said, "Yes, but your wife Sarah will bear you a son, and you will call him Isaac. I will establish My covenant with him as an everlasting covenant for his descendants after him" (Gen. 17:18-19).

Although Esau was Isaac's firstborn, the Lord confirms the covenant to Jacob (Gen. 35:11-12) and reiterates it often throughout psalms and the prophets (Psalm 105:8-11; Amos 9:14-15). One of the most compelling passages is found in Jeremiah 31; in this prophecy, the permanence of Israel's nationhood is irrevocably established.

> This is what the LORD says, he who appoints the sun to shine by day who decrees the moon and starts to shine by night, who stirs up the sea so that its waves roar, the Lord Almighty is his name: "Only if these decrees vanish from my sight," declares the LORD, "will the descendents of Israel ever cease to be a nation before me... Only if the heavens above can be measured and the foundations of the earth be searched out, will I reject all the descendents of Israel because of all that they have done," declares the LORD (Jer. 31:35-37).

The Judgments on Israel

Although the land grant to Abraham and the Messianic promises were unconditional, the Law of Moses given at Mt. Sinai was a conditional covenant. This simply means that the Israelites had a responsibility to keep their part of the covenant. The Lord would do His part, but He would not do their part, which was obedience and faithfulness to Him.

Before continuing, let us remember that the Apostle Paul wrote to the Galatians that the unconditional promise was given 430 years before the Law of Moses; Paul reasons that therefore, the promise of the original covenant with Abraham is not nullified by the later, conditional covenant with Moses (Gal. 3:17-18).

The Torah describes in much detail the abundant rewards for obedience and the horrific consequences of disobedience (Lev. 26; Deut. 28). The chronicles of Israel's history and the extensive warnings of the prophets tell the heartbreaking story of Israel's idolatry and disobedience to the Lord, with some notable righteous and encouraging exceptions. These witnesses still speak through our Scriptures as a testimony to the unfaithfulness of my people and the faithfulness of God to His unchanging Word.

All that was spoken by the prophets came upon Israel, and in His righteous judgments, the Lord used pagan Gentile empires to execute cruel and ruthless punishments upon His own people. The primary national calamities were executed by Assyria near the end of the eighth century B.C.; Babylon in 586 B.C.; and Rome under Vespasian in 70 A.D. As a result of each of these sequential judgments, the Jewish inhabitants of Israel were killed in the tens of thousands and exiled to distant countries; in the second two judgments, the Lord's temple and city were trampled upon by Gentile empires until the days of the promised restoration would come (Luke 21:24).

The Lord Yeshua prophesied to His own people of the severe judgments which would fall within one generation of His death and resurrection.

> *When you see Jerusalem being surrounded by armies, you will know that its desolation is near. For this is the time of punishment in fulfillment of all that has been written. How dreadful it will be in those days for pregnant women and nursing mothers! There will be great distress in the land and wrath against this people. They will fall by the sword and will be taken as prisoners to all the nations. Jerusalem will be trampled on by the Gentiles until the times of the Gentiles are fulfilled (Luke 21:20, 22-24).*

Even as our Lord was staggering under the weight of His cross toward His own crucifixion, torn and bleeding from scourging, He was not thinking of

Himself; He was concerned about the coming holocaust of His children, telling them not to weep for Him, but for themselves and their children (Luke 23:28-31).

Forty years after our Lord spoke these words, the Roman Empire wrought the most merciless destruction against the land, the people of Israel, and the city of Jerusalem. In a few short years, the Jewish people lost their nationhood and institutions, their temple and sacrificial system which God had commanded, their land and the capital city where He had placed His name, and the blood of more than a million sons and daughters.

The details of this cruelty and desolation would be more than most readers could bear. Likewise, if the dangers facing our own nation were perceived and understood, no spiritual price would seem too high to prevent such irrevocable calamity from befalling the ones we love.

Paul alerts us that the judgments suffered by Israel were written as a warning to the church, to serve as an example of His severity (1 Cor. 10:11). He writes to the Gentile believers in Rome, concerning God's judgments upon the Jews:

> *Do not be arrogant, but be afraid. For if God did not spare the natural branches, he will not spare you either* (Rom. 11:20b-21).

Replacement Theology

Due to the harshness of punishments that befell the Jewish people, particularly those after the crucifixion of Yeshua, a theology of God's rejection of Israel began to take shape during the second century by the leaders of the Gentile church, after the original Jewish apostolic community had died off. There were other reasons for this development: for reasons of self-protection, the Gentile believers wished to distance themselves from Roman persecution of Jews; the rise of the influence of Greek thought led to an allegorical (symbolic) method of interpreting the Scriptures; and a spirit of anti-Semitism influenced and encouraged Christians to disdain the Jews.

For an in-depth scriptural study of the relationship between the Church, the nation of Israel, and the Jewish people, as well as the Lord's restoration of all things in these last days, read *Israel, the Church and the Last Days*.[23] This is one of the most scholarly, comprehensive and biblically balanced books written on this subject. For a more prophetic and evangelistic perspective, visit the ministry of Messianic Vision, directed by Sid Roth. His book, *The Race to Save the World*[24] provides a concise picture of God's heart on this vital topic. I believe that Sid is a highly anointed end-time spokesman, whom God has appointed to refute the powerful deception of Replacement Theology.

To this day, Replacement Theology is widespread among the professing church; this position essentially states that Israel was formerly chosen by God for His redemptive purposes but is no longer prophetically significant. Since the majority of the Jewish nation rejected the Lord Jesus as the Messiah, the blessings promised to Israel have been removed and given to His new chosen people, "the church." Thus, according to this theology, the church has replaced Israel as the recipient of God's favor and promises; the Jewish people are tragically destined to fulfill the negative aspects of God's Word: cursing, eternal wandering, deserving of mistreatment at the hands of the nations, and the status of a people out of favor with God, without a hopeful future.

During the eighteen centuries that the Jewish people were dispersed throughout the earth, a number of Gentile church fathers taught that the Jews would never again inhabit the land of their forefathers, and that God had no more future redemptive purposes for the physical seed of Abraham, Isaac and Jacob.

When the State of Israel was reborn in 1948 out of the ashes of the holocaust, many Christians from this theological camp had a change of heart. They recognized the staggering reality that after nearly 1900 years of exile, the scattered Jewish people were returning to their original territory which had been promised to their fathers.

Even so, many still claim that this event was merely a political accident, rather than a divine fulfillment of biblical prophecy. After all, the Jewish people who returned to the newly reborn State of Israel were not "born again Christians," and many believers could not grasp God's sovereign move in the lives of those who did not yet acknowledge Yeshua. However, a number of Scriptures teach that the Lord Almighty is sovereign over the hearts of those who do not know Him; one such example is found in Isaiah:

> *I will lead the blind by ways they have not known, along unfamiliar paths I will guide them... Hear, you deaf; look, you blind and see! Who is blind but my servant, and deaf like the messenger I send? Who is blind like the one committed to me, blind like the servant of the LORD?* (Is. 42:16a, 18-19)

There are innumerable Scriptures which demonstrate that the Lord is faithful to His covenant promises, even when His people are unfaithful. If the Church can easily believe this about herself, can she not believe it for Israel? Ezekiel declares that it is not for Israel's sake that the Lord fulfills His promises; it is for the sake of His name and His reputation as a covenant-keeping God among the nations (Ezek 36:22-28). Isaiah and Jeremiah contain many examples of the Lord's faithfulness.

The Salvation of Israel

The Torah, Psalms and Prophets are full of God's faithfulness to fulfill His covenants with the Jewish people, but what does the New Testament say about this matter? Let us examine Paul's foundational teaching epistle to the Romans. In Chapters 9-11, Paul turns his full attention to God's dealings with his "own race," the physical seed of Abraham, Isaac and Jacob. In Chapter 9, Paul teaches on the "election" of certain people by God, namely, His sovereign choices. Paul's intercessor's heart is willing to give up his own salvation for the sake of his physical brothers and sisters, the Jewish people!

> I have great sorrow and unceasing anguish in my heart. For I could wish that I myself were cursed and cut off from Christ for the sake of brothers, those of my own race, the people of Israel. Theirs is the adoption as sons; theirs the divine glory, the covenants, the receiving of the law, the temple worship and the promises. Theirs are the patriarchs, and from them is traced the human ancestry of Christ, who is God over all, forever praised! Amen (Rom. 9:2-5).

He continues that although Abraham had two sons, it was through Isaac that the promise was given; likewise, Rebekah gave birth to twins, and yet before they were even born, God had already chosen Jacob over his older twin, Esau. "Jacob I loved, but Esau I hated" (Rom. 9: 13).

Of course, the Lord knew that Esau would despise his birthright as the first-born and would choose to fill his belly with one meal in exchange for his inheritance from God; Jacob, on the other hand, would covet the favor of God and the heritage of the firstborn, even though he would pay a huge earthly price for this unseen reward of divine blessing.

In Romans 9:30-10:21, Paul laments the unbelief of his people and shares his fervent prayer that Israel might be saved. He reiterates the necessity of heart-felt faith for salvation, available to both Jew and Gentile and highlights Moses' prophecy that God will make the Jewish people envious by those who are "not a nation."

As clearly stated in the gospels and Acts, the disciples and apostles were Jews; the first tens of thousands saved in the early apostolic preaching were Jews (Acts 21:20, 2:41, 4:4, 5:14), including many priests (Acts 6:7). Nevertheless, the majority of Israel and her religious leadership did not accept Yeshua as the Messiah, and Paul was severely persecuted by his former Pharisaic brothers and colleagues in the Sanhedrin.

Despite the fact that much of the Jewish leadership rejected the claims of the Lord Yeshua, Paul asks and answers two questions in the Roman letter, whose purposes are to affirm God's continuing faithfulness to the Jewish people:

I ask then: Did God reject his people? By no means! I am an Israelite myself, a descendant of Abraham from the tribe of Benjamin. God did not reject his people, whom he foreknew (Rom. 11:1-2a).

Did they stumble so as to fall beyond recovery? Not at all! Rather, because of their transgression, salvation has come to the gentiles, to make Israel envious (vs. 11).

Paul's desire is to maximize his ministry to the Gentiles in order to provoke his own people to envy and reap their salvation. He begins to reveal the mystery of the inclusion of the Gentiles into the covenants, which he likens to an olive tree. Paul had described this same mystery to the Ephesians, where he depicted the gentile believers as "being brought near to the commonwealth of Israel, and being joint heirs with Israel" (Eph 2:12-13, 3:6).

The rabbinic apostle then compares the spiritual heritage of his people to a cultivated olive tree: "If the root is holy, so are the branches" (Rom. 11:16). Paul portrays the Gentile believers as "wild" olive branches, who have been grafted into this cultivated tree and who share in the nourishing sap from the root. He then explains that some of the natural branches have been broken off of the tree due to unbelief. Paul warns the "grafted in" branches not to be arrogant or boast over the natural branches because "You do not support the root, but the root supports you" (vs. 17-18, 20).

After carefully building this analogy, Paul concludes that God is willing and able to bring the Jewish people back into their own olive tree if they will renounce unbelief and turn their hearts to Yeshua as Messiah and Lord. This natural olive tree represents a sweeping panorama of covenantal relationship and blessings: the gift of eternal life through the blood of Yeshua, the Passover Lamb; the adoption as sons and daughters into God's family; the inclusion into the holy offices of prophet, priest and king in union with the Lord Jesus (Joel 2:28, 1Pet 2:5, Rev 2:26-27, 5:10, 20:6); and the fruitful heritage promised to Abraham, Isaac and Jacob.

The unconditional land grant of the territory of Israel was primarily intended for the physical offspring, although the Lord will draw many of His own ones from the nations to inhabit the Land as well (Isa 49: 22-23, 56:6-8, 60:10).

The Gentile believers, through faith in Yeshua, have been grafted into this most desired tree and receive all the blessings and promises afforded by the nourishing sap from the root. In exactly the same way, Jewish believers who are connected by the same faith in Yeshua to their own original tree, receive the full measure of the blessings and promises of our loving Father.

If they do not persist in unbelief, they will be grafted in, for God is able to graft them in again. After all, if you were cut out of an olive tree that is wild by nature, and contrary to nature were grafted into a cultivated olive tree, how much more readily will these, the natural branches, be grafted into their own olive tree! (vs. 23-24)

Finally, Paul addresses God's sovereign plan to remove the Jewish hardness of heart at an appointed moment in history which he calls, "the fullness of the Gentiles" and prophesies the salvation of the Jewish people and the nation of Israel. Although his own people have persecuted him as "enemies," he affirms that for the sake of the patriarchs they are beloved because the "gifts and calling of God are irrevocable" (vs. 28-29).

His conclusion is that just as the Gentile believers have been shown mercy, they too must show love and mercy to the Jewish people, from whose tree they derive life and nourishment (vs. 30-31).

I do not want you to be ignorant of this mystery, brothers, so that you may not be conceited; Israel has experienced a hardening in part until the full number of the Gentiles has come in. And so all Israel will be saved, as it is written: "The deliverer will come from Zion; he will turn godlessness away from Jacob. And this is my covenant with them when I take away their sins." As far as the gospel is concerned, they are enemies on your account, but as far as election is concerned, they are loved on account of the patriarchs, for God's gifts and his call are irrevocable (vs. 25-29).

How Should Christians View the Jewish People?

The Apostle Paul has set a high standard for the behavior of the Gentile believers toward the Jewish people, from whom their faith and salvation sprang. It is tragic and outrageous that Christian nations and individuals have slandered, insulted and persecuted the Jews since the second century.

While one might expect beastly behavior from those outside of God's values, it is shameful and grievous to observe the blood-stained track record of Christian nations and their churches. This record includes: the libels of the Dark Ages, claiming that the Jews used Christian blood to bake matzoh; the European Crusaders burning Jews alive in Jerusalem's Great Synagogue; Spain's religious leaders conducting torture and murder during the Inquisition; the Russian campaigns of murder, beatings, rape and the burning of Jewish villages, called pograms; and Christian Germany's gas chambers and chimneys of human ash during the genocide of Adolph Hitler.

Despite the frequent use of the name of Christ as justification for these atrocities, the Jewish Messiah will not permit His name to be associated with the beastly savagery committed by these and other nations and individuals;

whatever these professing Christians did to His brothers, they have done to Him (Matt. 25:31-46).

Without repentance, any nation and its churches which participated in, or remained silent during these atrocities, will pay a price too great to bear when the grapes of wrath are finally gathered into the winepress of God's fury.

Paul writes, "Salvation has come to the Gentiles to make Israel envious." Has the behavior of the Christian Church made the Jewish people envious throughout history? In fact, the behavior of the visible, institutional church, both Catholic and Protestant, has driven the Jewish people further from Messiah. Out of ignorance of Scripture, cultural arrogance and anti-Semitism, the historically visible church has sometimes portrayed Jesus Christ as a Gentile Savior who is unrelated to the Hebraic heritage, bloodline, or spiritual practices. Much of the professing church has also failed to realize the chilling truth about the Sheep and the Goats: how much weeping and irrevocable remorse there will be on the day we appear before the Throne of the King of Israel if we have despised His own kith and kin!

In these last days, the Lord Yeshua is restoring to the true church His original identity and His broken heart of yearning and love for Israel. The Lord's sons and daughters from among the nations are now open to the corrective voice of their Messiah Yeshua, the Son of David. The title "Son of David" is a royal title, reserved in Scripture for the coming King, Messiah alone. Is Yeshua indeed the King of the Jews? Those who crucified Him knew that He was; does His own church know this?

Some preachers claim that Jesus Christ was born a peasant, citing that on the day of his purification, His parents were only able to sacrifice two doves, rather than a lamb and a dove (Luke 2:22-24; Lev. 12:2-8). Surely, the Lord Yeshua was not a peasant, for this denies His kingly lineage! Our Lord was a royal son of David and descended from the kingly tribe of Judah on both parental trees.

It is true that it was not appointed for Him to be raised in luxury. Even so, He was born a King (Matt. 2:1-2); recognized immediately by Nathaniel as the King of Israel (John 1:49); acknowledged as King by a significant segment of Israel during His earthly ministry (John 6:14-15; Matt. 21:9); and died a King, for even His enemies declared His Kingship on the wretched tree where He was hung (Matt. 27:37). In these five "witnesses" of His kingship, notice that the first and the last examples are Gentile recognition of His kingship, and the second, third and fourth examples are Jewish recognition of His kingship. Thus, the matter is fully established by the mouths of Jew and Gentile alike.

The mouth of the Lord Jesus Himself is the ultimate witness: from the first verse in the New Testament to the final words of Revelation, the Lord identifies

Himself as the Son of David, forever linking His identity to His Jewish brethren (Matt. 1:1; Rev. 22:16).

The Lord will always have a witness on the earth, and there has always been a remnant of the church that has loved the Jewish people; these faithful ones believed that the Lord's Scriptural promises are not nullified, despite the blindness of the Jewish people to Yeshua's identity. Tragically, most of these brave Christians were killed for the crime of loving the Jews and defending the reliability of God's promises.

Francis Kett, a Fellow at Corpus Christi College at Cambridge, proposed that Israel would be regathered as a nation. He was burned at the stake in 1589 for this teaching.

The ten Boom family risked their lives to hide Jewish people from the Nazi campaign in Holland; they were punished with arrest and death in the cruel camps. Corrie survived to tell their testimony in *The Hiding Place.*

Christian theologian Dietrich Bonhoeffer opposed Hitler and was hanged in 1945. His letters from prison were later published as a book, *Prisoner for God,* in which he lamented that the German churches had lost their vitality and moral voice because they had not condemned Nazism and its practices.

Raoul Wallenberg was a Swedish diplomat to Hungary who used his influence and personal wealth to obtain Swedish passports for 20,000 Hungarian Jews during World War II; before the Soviet liberation of Budapest, Wallenberg convinced the Nazi's to cancel the planned slaughter of another 70,000 Jews. He was arrested by the Soviets in 1945, and the circumstances of his death remain a mystery.

Other heroes remain nameless, but our Lord knows their names and "rewards each one according to what they have done" (Matt. 16:27).

Located in the garden of Jerusalem's Holocaust Museum *Yad Vashem* is the "Avenue of the Righteous Gentiles." The people of Israel have planted a row of trees for each Gentile who gave his or her life to save Jewish lives. Although there are very few trees in this garden, each hero of faith is greatly honored and appreciated by the people of Israel. Heaven also honors the nameless martyrs, to the glory of God's faithfulness!

In these accelerated last days, the small remnant of the Church which has loved the Jewish people is now becoming a mighty army. Surely the Lord Yeshua is eager to restore His identity to His church, in order that they might fulfill the following purposes of His heart: to comfort His people (Isa. 40:1-2); to make Israel envious, leading to their salvation (Rom 11:11); to have compassion on Zion and to pity her (Ps. 102:13-14); and to give the Lord no rest until He establishes Jerusalem and makes her the praise of the earth (Isa. 62:6-7).

You will arise and have compassion on Zion, For it is time to show favor to her;
the appointed time has come. For her stones are dear to your servants; her very
dust moves them to pity. For the LORD will rebuild Zion and appear in his glory.
He will respond to the prayer of the destitute; he will not despise their plea. Let
this be written for a future generation, that a people not yet created may praise the
LORD (Ps. 102:13-14, 16-18).

Interestingly, the phrase, "Let this be written for a future generation" could accurately be translated, "Let this be written for the last generation," as an examination of the Hebrew text reveals. Indeed, although God's Word is always true, these words are even more timely and relevant in this very generation, "upon whom the fulfillment of the ages has come" (1 Co. 10:11).

The Parable of Ruth and Naomi

In the previous chapter, we explored covenant friendship as exemplified by Ruth's loyalty to Naomi. Although the Book of Ruth describes an historical event, it is also a parable of the end-time church and Israel. Hidden under the surface of the story we find the Lord's standards for His church's treatment of the Jewish people and the great rewards for blessing them. The fulfillment of His redemptive purposes on earth is dependent on this strategic relationship. Let us now explore this parable.

In Leviticus 23, the Lord inserts a command between the spring feasts of the Lord and the fall feasts; this verse seems almost out of place:

When you reap the harvest of your land, do not reap to the very edges of your field
or gather the gleanings of your harvest. Leave them for the poor and the alien
[foreigner]. I am the Lord your God (Lev. 23:22).

The Israelites knew what it felt like to be living in a foreign land and dependent on the kindness of their hosts to obtain food. During their years in Egypt, they received their daily food rations at the mercy of their taskmasters and had no property of their own. They were slaves.

Knowing that His people would be granted their own land and properties, the Lord makes it very clear that the Israelite landowners must leave behind the gleanings of the fields for the poor. The foremen and harvesters are not to pick up every last kernel of grain, nor are they to gather the grapes a second time from their vineyards; they are to leave fruit behind for the needy sojourners in Israel. This merciful and kind provision in His Torah sets the stage for the story of Ruth and the grain fields of Boaz.

"Bethlehem" means "House of Bread" but ironically, the famine drives

Naomi's family to Moab for food. When the famine ends, Naomi and Ruth return to Bethlehem, and Ruth gleans in the fields to provide food for her mother-in-law. Ruth humbles herself and picks up the "crumbs" which fall from the Israeli table, which is the property of a Jewish landowner. Ruth had been instructed by Naomi about the legal privilege of a poor foreigner to glean from the field of the owner.

More than a thousand years later, a Canaanite woman approached the Lord Yeshua and pleaded with Him to heal her demon-possessed daughter (Matt. 15:21-28). He replied, "I was sent only to the lost sheep of Israel." As she continued to plead, He answered, "It is not right to take the children's bread and throw it to their dogs."

The Lord's answer to her was not a matter of prejudice but one of protocol. As Paul writes to the Romans, "[salvation is] first for the Jew, then for the Gentile" (Rom. 1:16).

The desperate woman's reply is so pleasing to the Lord that He is willing to grant her request. "Yes, Lord, but even the dogs eat the crumbs that fall from the master's table."

This persistent Gentile woman was willing to humble herself before the Jewish Messiah and acknowledge that even a crumb from the table of Israel's children would be enough to deliver and heal her daughter. She went away rejoicing, for she received what she needed from Yeshua that day, due to her humility and persistence.

While Ruth begins by gleaning "crumbs," her extraordinary loyalty to her Israeli mother-in-law becomes known to Boaz, the owner of the fields; he begins to show Ruth more generosity as time passes. Each time Ruth receives a greater gift from Boaz, she immediately takes the blessing back to Naomi. The blessings multiply, and Ruth shares the multiplication with Naomi in a cycle of reciprocal blessings: Israel (Boaz) blesses Ruth; Ruth then blesses Israel (Naomi). Ruth represents the end-time Gentile church: having originally received the Gospel from Israel's table, the church now needs to give back to the Jewish people, out of her storehouse of the bountiful mercy she has received (Rom. 11:30-31).

As wonderful as Boaz's generosity may have been, there was a dramatic shift in the landscape halfway through the story. As I was preparing to teach this material on Pentecost, the Lord spoke to my heart:

"What changed the equation from generosity to marriage? What was the key which transformed Boaz from being a very generous man to Ruth's husband?"

Since I did not know the answer, the Lord provided the key: *"Naomi taught Ruth the Torah, the Law of Moses; she explained to her the Law of the Kinsman-Redeemer. Naomi was not in a position to convince Boaz to consider marrying*

Ruth; rather, she sent her Moabite daughter-in-law to remind Boaz of his responsi-bilities according to the Law, as well as showing him the love in her heart. This would shift the equation from mere generosity to the full privileges of marriage."

I was overjoyed to receive this awesome key of understanding from the Lord, for my own sake as well as that of the teaching I was preparing.

When Ruth said to Boaz, "Spread the corner of your garment over me, for you are my Kinsman-Redeemer," she was citing the Law of Moses so that he would remember his legal responsibilities. As soon as he heard this, he replied that she was correct; however, there was one nearer relative than himself who had to be consulted.

The very next day, Boaz implemented the full civil and legal meetings and agreements; through this Boaz demonstrated that the nearest kinsman was not willing to marry Ruth and give her children, due to endangering his estate. The gracious and more generous Boaz was thus free to marry her and give her children in the name of Elimelech, Naomi's late husband.

When Ruth lay at Boaz's feet, two important changes took place in their re-lationship: she showed him her love through an intimate gesture, although no physical consummation took place that night; and she demonstrated her under-standing of the Torah, although a Moabite. Both her knowledge of the Law and her love of Boaz himself moved his heart deeply, and the matter would be set-tled within twelve hours.

Once Boaz married her, it was no longer a case of generosity to a foreigner; rather, Ruth became a Mother of Israel, with all of the full rights and property of her husband. As Ephesians explains, she became a full heir to all of the com-monwealth of Israel, grafted into the fullness of the blessings. The result of this marriage was the birth of the grandfather of King David and in the fullness of time, the birth of the Messiah, who would bring salvation to all the nations of the earth.

The Seeds of the Gospel Sown to the Nations

The Jewish apostles gave their lives to take the living bread of the Gospel to the nations. The Gentiles ate the life-giving kernels which fell from Israel's table; these were the gifts of salvation through faith in the risen Lord Yeshua, healing, deliverance and the infilling of the Holy Spirit. These overflowing blessings have been poured out generously upon the church. Just as Ruth's apron was heavy with many measures of Boaz's grain, so Messiah has spread out His tallit before Him, laden with life-giving seed for the nations. Even the crumbs contain resurrection power! The church has had nearly 2,000 years to bear the fruit of the good seed which was sown into their field by the Jewish apostles' words and blood.

The church must walk in Ruth's love and humility, continually bringing back the fruit of love and the seeds of spiritual life to Israel, her Naomi. The Messiah carefully observes the behavior of His church toward the Jewish people as Boaz observed Ruth's devotion, and he rewarded her accordingly. What will be our reward from Him? "I will bless those who bless you, and whoever curses you I will curse" (Gen. 12:3a).

The Bride is called to rest at Yeshua's feet in intimate devotion and pray, "Spread the corner of Your garment over me, for you are my Kinsman-Redeemer." As Ruth requested to be grafted into the people and covenants of Israel, so should the Church draw near to Israel in humility.

Through fervent intercession, she should "remind" her heavenly Boaz of His scriptural promises to His people, as Ruth reminded Boaz of his biblical responsibilities.

In Isaiah 62:6 we read, "You who call on the Lord, give yourselves no rest." The Hebrew text says, "You who remind the Lord, who bring to His remembrance, give yourselves no rest." This "reminder" word is the identical word for a "secretary" in modern Israel *(mazkirim)*. It is as if the Lord is saying that intercessors are like secretaries who remind the Boss of His divine appointments with destiny!

While the Lord does not have a problem with His memory, He rewards intercession in which His people reason with Him from knowledge of Scripture and bring to His remembrance what He promised. We see this intercessor's "reminder" function often in the prayers of Moses and the prophets. Isaiah describes the role of the "watchmen" as those who remind the Lord continually:

> I have posted watchmen on your walls, O Jerusalem; They will never be silent, day or night. You who call on the LORD, give yourselves no rest, and give him no rest till he establishes Jerusalem and makes her the praise of the earth (Isa. 62:6-7).

Even the Lord's mother prayed this same way when she rejoiced at Elizabeth's house, early in her pregnancy. She declared that the Lord had remembered to be merciful to Abraham, as He had promised (Luke 1:54-55).

As the Church moves into her full maturity as a spotless and humble Bride, she will bless and cover the Jewish people with intercession and practical support. In response, the Kinsman-Redeemer will spread the corner of His garment over her and take her as His own Bride. As with Ruth and Boaz, the fruits of this marriage will be the salvation and restoration of the Jewish people; in the same way, Naomi's bitterness and desolation were exchanged for joy when her heritage was restored.

The birth of the son who was laid in Naomi's lap prepared the way for the King of kings. A bridal company is now being birthed who will do the works that the Lord Jesus did. These works will include healing, bringing good tidings to Zion, extending to the Jewish people mercy and good fruits and preparing the way for the return of the King of kings (John 14:12; Isa. 40:3,9; James 3:17).

As the true Church reaches maturity, the Messiah's character, good fruits and deeds are finally being seen by the Jewish people. Paul expressed this longing for the body of believers to come into maturity in Ephesians:

> ...*until we all reach unity in the faith and in the knowledge of the Son of God, and become mature, attaining to the whole measure of the fullness of Christ* (Eph. 4:13).

In the cycle of reciprocal blessings found in the book of Ruth, we see the gifts flowing from the Jews to the Gentiles and then from the Gentiles back to the Jews. This cycle will continue to produce a great harvest of salvation upon the earth. As the full maturity of the Gentile church will yield salvation and restoration for the Jewish people, so the salvation of the Jews will reap a great end-time harvest among the nations. Thus, the law of sowing and reaping is fulfilled according to the Lord's sovereign purposes: to bring His Yeshua (salvation) to the Jewish people and to the ends of the earth.

> *For if their rejection is the reconciliation of the world, what will their acceptance be but life from the dead?* (Rom. 11:15)

Why Do the Nations Rage?

Surely there are many majestic capitals in this world with greater wealth, beauty and resources than the city of Jerusalem. Where are her great rivers or mineral wealth? Where are her magnificent boulevards? Where is her port or her commercial center of finance, investments and stock trading? Where are the smooth and powerful bankers and politicians who use their great wealth and influence to shape international policies and world economic trends?

These are not found in Jerusalem, for her beauty is hidden from the eyes and standards of this world. As Esther remained a humble Jewish orphan, hidden from the eyes of Persia until the time came for her to be revealed, so Jerusalem waits for the revealing of her glory to the nations.

Despite her lack of worldly value, she is the most contested piece of real estate on the earth, although a small and dusty piece indeed. Every powerful nation seems to take an enormous interest in the ownership, inhabitancy and political status of Jerusalem, though one wonders why. "Why do the nations conspire, and the peoples plot in vain?" (Psalm 2:1)

I am going to make Jerusalem a cup that sends all the surrounding peoples reeling. On that day, when all the nations of the earth are gathered against her, I will make Jerusalem an immovable rock for all the nations. All who try to move it will injure themselves. On that day I will set out to destroy all the nations that attack Jerusalem (Zech. 12:2-3,9).

During the last nineteen hundred years, these words of Zechariah would have seemed strange indeed to anyone looking at the city with a natural eye. Since she was trampled upon by many foreign governments as the Lord Yeshua had prophesied, Jerusalem was a dismal and dirty town in the Syrian province of various empires, the most recent being the Ottoman Empire and the British.

In his book *Innocents Abroad* in 1869, author Mark Twain wrote about this city: "Rags, wretchedness, poverty and dirt, Jerusalem is mournful and dreary and lifeless. I would not desire to live here."

W. H. Bartlett wrote in 1842, "If the traveler can forget that he is treading on the graves of a people from whom his religion has sprung, on the dust of her kings, prophets and holy men, there is certainly no city in the world that he will sooner wish to leave than Jerusalem. Nothing can be more void of interest than her gloomy, half ruinous streets and poverty-stricken bazaars."

Colonel Condor wrote, in Amateur Archeology in 1897, "The 'Latin Kingdom' of Jerusalem is a very ugly city. It is badly built of mean stone, houses poised on the slope of the watershed, and seems in instant danger of sliding into the Kidron Valley."[25]

However, as the modern reader considers Zechariah's prophecy, the possibility of an imminent international assault on Jerusalem seems very likely, due to the frenzied political climate which surrounds this city. It seems that every powerful nation and major religious groups seek to stake a claim on this city; somehow, she is desired as the International City or the City of All World Religions. What could explain this odd phenomenon, since she still retains little worldly wealth or value?

But Now I Have Chosen Jerusalem

The only explanation for the nations' intense desire to claim or rule Jerusalem is that the Sovereign Lord has claimed it for Himself and has assigned Jerusalem to be the past, present and future site of His redemptive acts throughout human history. Thus, those who are in rebellion against the King of kings will wish to rule or damage the city to which He will return, in order to disrupt His redemptive purposes. "This is Jerusalem, which I have set in the center of the nations" (Ezek. 5:5).

It was to Mount Moriah, one of the mountains of Jerusalem, that the Lord led Abraham and his son Isaac on a three-day journey. The Lord had commanded Abraham to offer up his only son, despite the promise of descendents to come from this same son. When they reached the mountain the Lord showed them, Abraham bound his son on the altar and lifted up the knife to slay him; the angel of the Lord stopped him and said, "I swear by Myself, declares the Lord, that because you have done this and have not withheld your son, your only son, I will surely bless you and make your descendants as numerous as the stars in the sky and as the sand on the seashore" (Gen. 22:16-17a).

It was the Lord who chose this location for Abraham's test of obedience and from this point onward, the Lord has continually chosen this city as the dwelling place for His name and His earthly reign. King David conquered this city from the Jebusites and established his kingdom here. The Psalmist wrote:

> For the LORD has chosen Zion, he has desired it for his dwelling: This is my resting place forever and ever (Psalm 132:13-14a).

David's son, Solomon was appointed by God to build the temple where God's glory would dwell. After completing his work, Solomon prayed and sacrificed to the Lord, and multitudes of musicians raised their voices in praise to God. The Lord affirmed His choice of Jerusalem, and His glory filled the temple.

> When Solomon finished praying, fire came down from heaven and consumed the burnt offering and the sacrifices, and the glory of the LORD filled the temple (2 Chr. 7:1).

"Baruch haBa b'Shem Adonai"— Blessed is He Who Comes in the Name of the Lord.

When the infant Yeshua was consecrated to the Lord as the first born male child, He was brought to Jerusalem. Every year, His parents went up to Jerusalem for the feasts (Luke 2:41). As a twelve-year-old boy, He remained behind in Jerusalem while His family began their trip home from the feast, causing concern to His parents. Yeshua explained to His parents that He had to be in His Father's house.

During the final week of His earthly ministry, the Lord rode into Jerusalem from the Mount of Olives. The whole crowd began to joyfully praise God for all the miracles they had seen (Luke 19:37):

> Hosanna to the Son of David! Blessed is he who comes in the name of the Lord! Hosanna in the highest! (Matt. 21:9b)

For the crowds of Israel to address Him as the "Son of David" was a clear declaration of His kingly identity and function. This unique and exalted title was reserved only for the Messiah, the Crown Prince of Israel. As the humble king approached Jerusalem and saw the city, He wept over it; so great was Messiah's love and heartbreak for this "city of God" which would not recognize the day of God's visitation (Luke 19:41-44). He wanted to gather her children under the shelter of His wings, but they were not willing; the price they would pay would be too grievous to bear (Matt. 23:37-39). He closes His lament over Jerusalem with this prophetic word:

> For I tell you, you will not see me again until you say, "Blessed is he who comes in the name of the Lord" (Matt. 23:39).

Who was the Lord addressing when He said, "You will not see Me again until…"? We know from Matthew 21:9 and John 12:13 that the Jewish crowds acknowledged Him as King when He rode into Jerusalem. In fact, the crowds cried out this very phrase: "*Baruch HaBa b'Shem Adonai!* Blessed is He who comes in the Name of the Lord!" It was not these joyful worshipers who condemned the Lord Yeshua to die.

The Lord knew that the time would come in the future when the religious leadership of Jerusalem would welcome Messiah with these words. His return to the city would be withheld until these words of love and welcome would be voluntarily and joyfully exclaimed!

I am so thankful that our Lord did not say, "You will never see Me again, Jerusalem!" Rather, He said, "You will not see Me again until you say, 'Blessed is He who comes in the Name of the Lord.'"

In saying, "until," the Lord is revealing that the city of Jerusalem will indeed see Him again at the time that she blesses Him and welcomes His appearing.

International worship leader Paul Wilbur has recently taught on a word from the Lord concerning Yeshua's prophetic signpost to Jerusalem.[26] If the crowds already proclaimed these words of welcome when He rode into Jerusalem before His death, from whom does the Lord require them before He returns to this city? Paul Wilbur discloses that it was to the Sanhedrin that Yeshua was speaking this prophetic word; this was the ruling council of seventy-one elders, primarily Pharisees and Sadducees. In the last days, there will need to be a functioning Sanhedrin in modern Jerusalem for this event to be fulfilled.

Paul Wilbur disclosed in a recent interview with Sid Roth that, in the last few years, the Sanhedrin has been reconvened in Jerusalem, thus paving the way for this critical welcome and recognition of Yeshua by the religious leaders of the Jewish people to take place.

A short time after the Lord's resurrection and ascension, Peter would stand in the Temple courts and tell the crowds of Jewish worshipers that their people acted in ignorance, as did their leaders in rejecting Messiah; he urged them to repent, adding:

He [Yeshua] must remain in heaven until the time comes for God to restore everything, as he promised long ago through his holy prophets" (Acts 3:17,19,21).

In other words, we will not see Him return to this city He loves until our people, specifically the spiritual leaders of our people, welcome the One who comes in the Name of the Lord! May He hasten the day of this joyous and overdue welcome. Amen.

I Have Installed My King in Zion

I believe in the literal return of the Lord Jesus Christ and in His future reign from the city of Jerusalem; this doctrine is strongly supported by Scripture. I can only present a few examples of this evidence, but further study will uphold this doctrine.

Then the man brought me to the gate facing east, and I saw the glory of the God of Israel coming from the east. The glory of the LORD entered the temple through the gate facing east. Then the Spirit lifted me up and brought me into the inner court, and the glory of the LORD filled the temple. He said, "Son of man, this is the place of my throne and the place for the soles of my feet. This is where I will live among the Israelites forever" (Ezek. 43:1a,4-5,7a).

This passage is part of a lengthy prophecy in which Ezekiel gives great detail about the temple which will be built in the latter days, as the prophet was shown in a vision; this temple has never yet been built in Jerusalem. The last nine chapters of Ezekiel are about the restoration of Jerusalem and the new temple which the Lord will inhabit.

Psalm 2 declares that the King of Israel will reign in Jerusalem and calls the Lord, "the Son." The nations are angry and rebel against His authority, for He rules with a rod of iron. In this passage, the psalmist asks: "Why do the nations rage?" God's answer to their rebellion is found in the establishment of His Anointed One in Zion. What will be the outcome of these rebellious nations when the Holy One's wrath is kindled?

Why do the nations conspire, and the peoples plot in vain? I have installed my King on Zion, My holy hill. Kiss the Son, lest he be angry, and you be destroyed in your way, for his wrath can flare up in a moment. Blessed are all who take refuge in him (Psalm 2:1,6,12).

Zechariah prophesies that after the terrible onslaught in which all the nations attack Jerusalem, the Lord's feet will stand on the Mount of Olives; this is the same mountain from which His pierced feet ascended nearly 2,000 years ago. The book of Acts tell us, "This same Jesus, who has been taken from you into heaven, will come back in the same way you have seen Him go into heaven" (Acts 1:11). Surely, the Lord is returning to Jerusalem, as He promised!

> *On that day his feet will stand on the Mount of Olives, east of Jerusalem. On that day, living water will flow out from Jerusalem, half to the eastern sea and half to the western sea, in summer and in winter. The LORD will be king over the whole earth. On that day there will be one LORD and his name the only name. Then the survivors from all the nations that have attacked Jerusalem will go up year after year to worship the King, the LORD Almighty and to celebrate the Feast of Tabernacles. If any of the peoples of the earth do not go up to Jerusalem to worship the King, the LORD Almighty, they will have no rain* (Zech. 14:4a,8-9,16-17).

Notice that at that time, not only Jews, but all the nations will be required to go up and celebrate the Feast of Tabernacles or they will not receive rain for the coming year. The Jewish people always begin to pray for the fall rains on Tabernacles, which is necessary for the spring harvest. Even if these Jews live in a part of the earth where rain is abundant, their hearts and prayers are connected to the dry and thirsty Land of Israel, and they faithfully pray for rain.

The nations will worship the Lord in Jerusalem, year after year during the Feast of Tabernacles. Since this passage in Zechariah takes place immediately after His feet land on the Mount of Olives, I believe this is a description of the thousand-year earthly reign of Messiah described in Revelation 20:1-6.

The Lord Yeshua says that to him who overcomes, He will give authority over the nations; He continues by quoting Psalm 2, concerning the Messiah's authority to rule the nations with a rod of iron (Rev. 2:26; Ps. 2:9). In other words, the Lord will delegate His authority to His own overcoming ones, who will reign over the nations with Him.

In the following passage, Isaiah describes the glory of the Lord covering Jerusalem; the images of the cloud by day and the fire by night remind us of the glory of the Lord covering the Israelites in the desert (Ex. 13:21-22).

In the verses preceding this passage, Isaiah makes reference to the "survivors" in Jerusalem who have been purified by a spirit of judgment and a spirit of fire. It seems that much calamity has again befallen this city before this glorious fulfillment takes place. This is in agreement with Zechariah's prophecy in which the nations come against Jerusalem to destroy her but are themselves destroyed by the Lord (Zech. 12:1-3).

> *Then the LORD will create over all of Mount Zion and over those who assemble there a cloud of smoke by day and a glow of flaming fire by night; over all the glory will be a canopy. It will be a shelter and shade from the heat of the day, and a refuge and hiding place from the storm and rain* (Isa. 4:5-6).

Truly, these are mere samples of the biblical passages which testify and confirm the doctrine of the Lord's earthly reign from the city of Jerusalem. As did the Bereans (Acts 17:11), each reader should carefully search the Scriptures to see if these things are true. If the Lord has spoken these words and if He meant them as the plain text declares, His Spirit will be gracious to confirm it to any who ask for understanding.

The voice of the prophets has spoken: Yeshua has prophesied that one day our people will welcome Him into Jerusalem as King; Paul has told us that all Israel will be saved; David writes that God has installed Messiah as King in Zion; Isaiah predicts that the Tabernacle of the Lord will cover the glory cloud over Jerusalem; Zechariah proclaims that the King will reign over the whole earth from Jerusalem; Ezekiel declares that the "soles of His feet" will dwell in Jerusalem with His people forever.

How will this change of heart take place? What will cause the Jewish people to look expectantly to Him and to "love His appearing"? Surely, some enormous change in the spiritual landscape will prompt Israel to say, "Baruch HaBa b'Shem Adonai! Blessed is He who comes in the Name of the Lord!"

The secret of this Jewish revival lies in the story of Joseph, the beloved one rejected by his brothers.

Joseph, a Hebrew in a Foreign Land

Q: When is a Jewish person not recognized by his own brothers as a Jew?

A: When he has spent decades, centuries or millennia in a foreign culture, language and people group. In Genesis 37, we read that Joseph's jealous brothers conspired to kill him because of the great favor that was upon this beloved son of Jacob. They ended up selling him as a slave into Egypt where he underwent terrible and unjust persecution. Throughout this time of servitude, suffering and wrongful imprisonment, he maintained his integrity and love of the Lord.

His righteousness was finally rewarded. Due to the supernatural ability given by God to interpret Pharaoh's prophetic dreams, Joseph became the most powerful man in Egypt. Pharaoh's dream prophesied seven years of famine, and the Lord gave to Joseph the authority and wisdom to prepare the entire nation for this coming famine by conducting a comprehensive national program of stockpiling grain.

Jacob and Joseph's eleven brothers experienced famine in the Land of Israel, and ten of the brothers went down to Egypt, seeking to buy food. Jacob had long since mourned the falsely reported death of Joseph, and his last remaining comfort was Benjamin, the youngest child; this boy was born to his beloved Rachel, who died giving birth to him.

When the ten brothers approached this Egyptian dignitary to request grain, they did not recognize their fully grown, clean-shaven brother. He had been groomed in the customs of Egypt and had matured into an imposing and noble Egyptian, bearing little resemblance to the Hebrew youth whom they had tormented and betrayed. He recognized his brothers immediately, and his tender heart shattered within, but he maintained his outward composure.

Joseph then implemented a series of tricks and traps for the brothers, not in order to harm them, but to cause them to repent of their secret act of treachery. This lengthy ruse proved psychologically damaging to the brothers and agonizing for Joseph, who could barely contain the flood of tears stored up in his tender heart.

In the end, the sight of his younger brother Benjamin caused the years of mental anguish and the fullness of his emotional grief to break open. He revealed his identity to his terrified and guilty brothers, and released a heartbreaking torrent of wailing; the pain of betrayal and the joy of restoration finally were permitted their full expression in this gentle soul.

Restoring the Lord's Identity

Joseph proved to be a righteous, merciful and forgiving brother to his sinful family. He was faithful to them despite their grotesque unfaithfulness to him. But why did they not recognize him? Joseph, the suffering servant, was in a foreign land among a foreign people. He spoke a different language and was the master of another nation. He did not look Jewish because of years of absorption into another culture. They did not know he was their brother, and when they recognized him, they were ashamed and grieved over their mistreatment of such a noble and generous ruler.

This is exactly how it will be when my people recognize their Jewish brother, Yeshua as the One they rejected. They will mourn, and He will be faithful to weep with them and restore them into the bond of brotherhood.

And I will pour out on the house of David and the inhabitants of Jerusalem a spirit of grace and supplication. They will look upon me, the one they have pierced, and they will mourn for him as one mourns for an only child, and grieve bitterly for him as one grieves for a firstborn son. On that day a fountain will be opened to the house of David and the inhabitants of Jerusalem, to cleanse them from sin and impurity (Zech. 12:10, 13:1).

The Lord Jesus has, in some sense, spent close to 2,000 years among the nations. His identity, name and image were altered after the death of the Jewish apostles, such that He is virtually unrecognizable as a Jewish Messiah to His own brothers. In the early years, this reshaping of the Lord's image was a deliberate series of theological and political decisions made by several generations of church fathers.

Over many centuries, the church perpetuated this "Gentile" version of Jesus, even an anti-Semitic Jesus, at times. The Protestant Reformers brought much praiseworthy restoration to the church, and a tremendous awakening occurred as Christians were able to learn and understand the Scriptures and the message of salvation by faith in the Lord Jesus. Even so, one vital restoration did not take place at the time of the Protestant Reformation: the restoration of the Lord's Jewish identity and His fathomless affection for His Jewish people.

Traditions and translations, pride and prejudice, and a lack of scriptural depth have produced a professing church which is cut off from the roots of the natural Olive Tree. Many fine scholars, such as Dan Juster and David Stern, have addressed this subject in detail, and I need not duplicate these efforts.

In these last days, the Lord is restoring all things (Acts 3:21). One of the things He is eager to restore is His original identity as the Son of David, Israel's most beloved King. Truly, He is the Lion of the Tribe of Judah from where we derive the word "Jew."

The Lord Yeshua will never turn His loving gaze away from His Bride, whom He has gathered under His wings from all the nations on earth. She is ever in His heart, which contains unlimited quantities of love to bestow on His own ones.

Even so, after nearly 2,000 years, He will now turn His gaze back to the land and city in which He has invested His name and reputation, and to the people from whom He originated. The Lord must complete His redemptive work in the people of Israel as He has promised through His prophets, through Paul and in His own declarations. The Jewish Messiah, like Joseph, must be recognized by his brothers!

This is what the Sovereign LORD says: It is not for your sake, O house of Israel, that I am going to do these things, but for the sake of my holy name, which you have profaned among the nations where you have gone. For I will take you out of the nations; I will gather you from all the countries and bring you back into your own land. I will sprinkle clean water on you, and you will be clean.

I will give you a new heart and put a new spirit in you; I will remove from you your heart of stone and give you a heart of flesh. And I will put my Spirit in you and move you to follow my decrees and be careful to keep my laws.

My dwelling place will be with them; I will be their God, and they will be my people. Then the nations will know that I the LORD make Israel holy, when my sanctuary is among them forever (Ezek. 36:22; 24-25a; 26-27; 37:27-28).

The Lord is laying it upon the heart of many who love Him to pray for the salvation of Israel and to pray for the peace of Jerusalem. This is not referring to a political peace or a false sense of negotiated security with the nations; rather, the peace of Jerusalem will only come as a result of a restored relationship with the Holy One of Israel and His Anointed One, the Lord Yeshua.

He is asking His Bride to show favor, mercy and compassion upon Zion and upon the Jewish people scattered throughout the earth. Without the prayers and covering of a compassionate church, the Jewish people will become prey for the ravenous beasts who seek to devour her, as is already happening in Russia and Europe. In addition, the nation of Israel is terribly vulnerable to the enmity and destructive plans of the nations around her; such are sheep without a shepherd, and only a loving expression from the Body of Messiah can bring back the lost sheep of Israel into the safety of the sheepfold.

Rejoice with Jerusalem and be glad for her, all you who love her; Rejoice greatly with her, all you who mourn over her. For you will nurse and be satisfied at her comforting breasts; you will drink deeply and delight in her overflowing abundance. As a mother comforts her child, so will I comfort you; and you will be comforted over Jerusalem (Isa. 66:10-11,13).

May the Lord confirm these written words by His Spirit, and may they bear the fruit of fervent love and intercession for the salvation of the Jewish people. If the Lord has called you to be a "watchman on the walls" (Isa. 62:6-7), may you speak and pray this end-time message before the nations and declare the Lord's covenant-keeping faithfulness to the Bride of Messiah! Amen.

RECEIVING ETERNAL SALVATION

If you have doubts about where your soul stands with God, or have never made a heartfelt decision to accept the salvation and atonement offered by Yeshua's (Jesus Christ's) sacrifice, then this section of the book is written expressly for you.

The God who created the heavens and the earth, as described in the Book of Genesis, calls Himself by numerous titles and names. His covenant Name is the Hebrew Name "YAHVEH," best translated, "the God who IS and EXISTS, apart from created things." He also calls Himself our Father, our King and the Husband of His people. He is the God who is called "The Father" in the writings of the New Testament.

The prophet Isaiah tells us that "all of us like sheep have gone astray; each has turned to his own way." There is not one who has been born on the earth who has not sinned and fallen short of the righteous standards of a pure and holy God.

When the Lord God saw that mankind would be forever cast away from His presence due to our sinful thoughts, words and deeds, He sent a part of Himself from heaven's glory to become flesh and blood, exactly like His earthly children. This part of Himself was always His Son, even before the creation of the universe. Even King David declared that God has a Son in Psalm 2. This was written one thousand years before Yeshua was born! This man is the only human who has never sinned in thought, word or deed, out of all the humans who have ever lived.

When this Holy Son was born of a Jewish virgin in Israel and became a human child, His given name was "Yeshua," which in Hebrew means "Salvation." We translate His name into many tongues, and in English, it is rendered, "Jesus." He will answer to His Name in *any* language!

In the Bible which is called "the Old Testament," the blood of animals was a necessary sacrifice to cover the sins of Israel's priests and individual worshipers. Only blood can atone for sin, according to Leviticus. However, the blood of animals was not of sufficient value to permanently remove sin from us. Therefore, the Son of God offered Himself as a spotless, sinless offering for the guilt of each and every one of us.

The Lord Jesus gave His life voluntarily. It seems that others took His life, but it was the Father's will and the Son's agreement to allow this great suffering and death to take place for our sakes. On the third day, He was raised from death to life, and this physical resurrection opened the gates of eternal life to all who follow Him with all of their hearts.

When we die, or when Yeshua returns to take His people and judge the world, we must face the righteous Judge. He has established the scales of eternal justice such that *no one* will be justified apart from the atoning death of His Son, Yeshua. No matter how "good" one's life is, no matter what religious tradition one lives under, both Jew and Gentile will be cast into hell for his or her personal sins unless they are made righteous and perfect by Yeshua's death and blood. There is no exception to this heavenly decree. Therefore, our only hope is to humble ourselves and accept the resurrected Lord Jesus Christ and His death as our personal covering, righteousness and entrance to Heaven. ("Christ" is the Greek word for "Messiah," which means, "Anointed One.")

When we pray to the Father to receive the forgiveness and atonement of His Son, the Holy Spirit of God comes to dwell in our spirits, and He never departs from us after this moment. In Hebrew, the Holy Spirit is called the *Ruach ha Kodesh*. He is the part of God who is able to be everywhere at the same time, and who searches our hearts at all times, knows all things about us and continually counsels and teaches us the will of God in our lives. He always glorifies the crucified and risen Lord Yeshua, and always speaks truth which is in perfect agreement with everything written in the Bible, both Old and New Covenants.

When we pray to receive Yeshua, we are also agreeing to lay down our rights, control and ownership of our lives. We are not "free" to deliberately indulge ourselves in any sinful word, thought or lifestyle. If He is not "Lord" of our lives, we have not understood who He is and what He has done. To receive Yeshua, the cost is our right to govern our own life and destiny. He has bought us with the price of His own blood, and if we want to hold onto our own rights, we cannot truly accept His purchase of our souls with His blood.

Please count the cost before you pray this prayer, because it is very serious business to make Jesus the Lord of your life. He might require your money, your time, your sleep, your choices, even your life. Almost all of the biblical writers were martyred for the Lord's sake; it is common in other nations today. However, the reward we will receive in heaven and the peace we receive on this earth so far outweigh these hardships that they will not be remembered when we see His face, smiling at us with favor and approval.

If you would like to receive the Lord Jesus now and be absolutely sure that your soul will be accepted as righteous when you face Him very soon, pray the following prayer (or a similar prayer) from the deepest place in your heart:

Dear Lord God, Creator of all things, I humble myself before You as a sinful person. I know I have sinned in my thoughts, words and deeds, and am not worthy to enter heaven based on my own righteousness or worthiness.

I know that You have always loved me, and have sent your Son Yeshua (or "Jesus") to die as a substitute for the punishment I deserve. I accept the sacrifice of His sinless blood which He shed for me on the cross as the atonement for my sins. I believe that You raised Him from the dead on the third day, that He now lives in heaven, and that I will be raised to life because of His victory over death. I ask for Your Holy Spirit to enter and fill me and change my life from this moment. I voluntarily surrender my rights and control of my life and choose to make You Lord of my life and destiny. I want to be with You forever in heaven, and I know that Yeshua's death and resurrection is the only way I can enter Your holy presence.

Thank You for so great a salvation, and the free gift of eternal life. I love you, Lord. In Yeshua's name I ask this, amen.

If you have sincerely prayed this prayer, you are now a new person, reborn in your spirit into His life of holiness, righteousness and love. Begin to read the Bible every day, both Old and New Testaments; it is especially important to read the gospels of Matthew, Mark, Luke and John to learn about Yeshua's ministry on earth. Begin to pray to Him every day. Talk to Him as you would talk to a friend, but with much love, reverence and respect for who His is. Find a church or Messianic congregation where the people truly love Yeshua and live in the power of His Holy Spirit. They will help you to grow in your new faith. The Lord will be with you, now and forever. Never deny Him, no matter what wicked men say to you or do to you, and you will receive eternal life.

EPILOGUE

JEALOUS LOVE

As I reflect on the stories, revelations and scriptural teachings in this book, I wonder if I have adequately conveyed the depth of my heart to the reader. How I hope that I fully expressed how worthy of our most passionate and whole-hearted love is this most precious, faithful, merciful and gentle Person, Yeshua.

I am a tremendously emotional person, and yet when I write, my words tend to be descriptive and somewhat factual. How can I leave this narrative without declaring my heart?

The Lord is a jealous God, a consuming fire. He will not settle for less than *all* of our heart, our devotion, our strength and intention. As odd as this might sound to those with families, He will not share us with anyone or anything. Yes, He will permit us to serve them, love them, pour out our time, prayers, patience and kindness upon them; but our hearts He will not share! His love for us is fierce, even frighteningly possessive. I doubt we can grasp the severity of His love for us, and I sense it would overwhelm us if we really knew.

The greatest commandment, according to our Lord's own Word is: "You shall love the Lord your God with all your heart, and all your soul and all your strength." Out of all the books and verses in the Bible, the Lord Jesus considers this to be the highest and most critical command. He will measure our lives by this greatest command, so why don't most Christians take it more seriously? The purpose for writing this book is to kindle the flames of consuming love in our hearts for Him, even as He burns with a jealous love for each one of us.

Earthly love is a two-way relationship. If one partner lavishes love on the other while the other just passively receives this love or passion, the lover is hurt or insulted. Love isn't something the husband does to the wife, nor is it something the wife does to the husband. They lavish love on each other in a mutual way with reciprocal affection, tenderness and passion. Where is the reciprocal love in our relationship with the Lover of our souls? Where is the other half of the love equation? We must lavish our love and worship upon Him, just as He generously pours out gracious love and blessings upon us.

Many books are written about the need for God's people to know Him, to know His thoughts and heartfelt concerns. We come to know Him through His written Word, and through the teaching and preaching of the Word. This is excellent and needful material. But where are the books written about how He must come to know us?

The Lord tells us that not only do His sheep know Him, but that He knows them as well (John 10:14,27). There are three chilling passages in Scripture which depict the Lord Jesus telling professing "Christians" that He never knew them!

> *But while they* [the five foolish virgins] *were on their way to buy the oil, the bridegroom arrived. The virgins who were ready went in with him to the wedding banquet. And the door was shut. Later the others also came. "Sir! Sir!"they said. "Open the door for us!" But he replied, "I tell you the truth, I don't know you"* (Matt. 25:10-12).

> *Many will say to me on that day, "Lord, Lord, did we not prophesy in your name, and in your name drive out demons and perform many miracles?" Then I will tell them plainly, "I never knew you. Away from me, you evildoers!"* (Matt. 7:22-23)

> *Once the owner of the house gets up and closes the door, you will stand outside knocking and pleading, "Sir, open the door for us." But he will answer, "I don't know you or where you come from." Then you will say, "We ate and drank with you, and you taught in our streets." But he will reply, "I don't know you or where you come from. Away from me, all you evildoers!"* (Luke 13:25-27)

The apostle Paul describes the difference between knowing and being known in this way:

> *The man who thinks he knows something does not yet know as he ought to know. But the man who loves God is known by God* (1 Cor. 8:3).

It is the Lord's primary intention for this book to highlight this life-changing truth and warning. We must voluntarily allow the Lord to know us intimately. While it is true that He already knows all the thoughts of every heart, He requires His children to be intimately and deeply open to Him, with full and transparent friendship and disclosure. Remember that, in Hebrew the verb "to know" connotes sexual intimacy between a husband and his wife, as it is written about Adam and Eve. The Lord Jesus is seeking spiritual intimacy with His beloved Bride. She must open her heart to Him freely and never hide her face or her voice from Him.

The Lord shares His secrets with His beloved friends. He expects no less from us. I pray that this book has ignited that transparency in each reader.

There is a holy jealously which burns for us in His passionate heart, and in some sense, we are meant to return the feelings to Him. Of course, we cannot "own" Him fully or keep Him all to ourselves! After all, He has millions of beloved children upon the earth and millions more in heaven, enjoying Him with the angels every day. He knows the stars by name and has a vast array of loved ones, purposes, and activities to conduct in the universe.

And yet He wants us to think of Him as "our very own Rock, our best friend, our dearest darling, our secret fortress and our only trusted confidant." For a brief moment, I can forget that He is simultaneously taking care of thousands of prayers, multiplied strategies, millions of angels, countless individual and corporate needs, the planetary and geological functions, and the preparations for the gathering of His Bride into the Wedding Feast. I can know that at this moment as I sit before Him, talking to Him about my most intimate thoughts, He has eyes and ears only for me.

The Lord can somehow treat each one of us as if we are the only person in the universe; we have one-hundred percent of His attention and nothing else matters. He loves us more than anyone or anything else at that moment. As Mike Bickle has said, "I am really beginning to believe that I am one of God's favorites! Now, that may sound arrogant to you until you understand that God has millions of favorites."[27]

I don't understand it, but I am sure He does this so that each one will feel like the most beloved, favored, blessed and adored child that has ever been loved in the history of mankind! He makes me feel this way, and I know He does this with all those who love Him.

Although everything He has is ours, I never feel that I have enough of Him. I often cry when nothing whatsoever is wrong, merely because I want much more of Him than I can see, hear or feel at this moment. I am always satisfied and always frustrated because I want to be with Him as He really is in the place where He really dwells. I never want to struggle again to know Him fully. But the struggle will continue until we have completed our race.

The journey with Yeshua on this earth is a faith walk. Blessed are those who have not seen, but believe. Blessed are those who love Him with all their heart, soul and strength. Blessed are those who trust in His goodness when they cannot feel His presence or sense His nearness. Blessed are those who trust in His goodness when He allows great suffering in their lives and many tears. Blessed are those who wait for the Lord, for He is worth waiting for!

All of Yeshua's love is yours, dearest reader. Give Him all of your love as well. Tell Him everything that is in your heart every day and in every circumstance. Although He knows the thoughts of your heart, He desires complete transparency. On that day, may you hear Him declare before the Father that you are His own one, and that He knows you.

Endnotes

1 Gregory, David. *Dinner with a Perfect Stranger*. Waterbrook Press, 2005.

2 Levergood, Carol. *YHVH'S Recipe*. Carol Levergood, 1997. Messages Direct, PO Box 360936, Melbourne, FL 32936-0936, Phone: 321-254-1477.

3 Schaeffer, Francis A. *Genesis in Space and Time*. Tyndale House Publishers, 1972.

4 See Chapter 10 for the complete biblical picture of Israel's salvation.

5 "The Art of Waiting on God." Sadhu Sundar Selvaraj. www.jesusministries.org

6 Gathering of Eagles Conferences sponsored by World for Jesus Ministries, www.worldforjesus.org

7 Goetz, Marty. From the CD: "The Love of God"

8 Davis, Paul Keith. *Books of Destiny* New Hampshire: Streams Publishing House, 2004.

9 Thomas, Choo. *Heaven is So Real*. Lake Mary, FL: Charisma House: A Strang Company, 2003.

10 Halkin, Abraham S., PhD. *201 Hebrew Verbs*. New York: Barron's Educational Series, 1970. Page 4: the feminine, present tense of the "Pu'al" form of "ahav" is "m'uhevet," and is translated, "to be in love."

11 See footnote in Chapter 4 for website information.

12 For more information on abortion, see www.prolife.com

13 To order Dr. Nathanson's book, *The Hand of God*, published by Regnery Publishing, Inc., call 1-800-858-3040.

14 Biographical material on Bernard Nathanson, M.D. is found at www.prolife.com/NATHAN.html

15 This shocking DVD, "Hard Truth" can be ordered from Heritage House at www.HH76.com or at 1-800-858-3040. Warning: a responsible parent or youth leader must view it before deciding whether a given child or youth group can handle this graphic material. It is also important to be sensitive to audiences which may contain women who have had abortions. This type of guidance is provided with the DVD.

16 This righteous ministry, under leadership of Stan and Leslie Johnson, issues warnings to our nation; www.prophecyclub.com. I particularly recommend the prophecies of Michael Boldea, the grandson of the late Romanian pastor, Dumitru Duduman, as well as those of Dumitru himself.

17 For Eagles' Wings or Pray for the Peace of Jerusalem, go to www.daytopray.com or call 1-800-51-WINGS.

18 Joyner, Rick. *The Call*. Morningstar Publications, 1999.

19 "iron plow": In the Book of Jasher, chapter 1, it is recorded that Cain

killed Abel with the iron part of the plowing instrument; see Joshua 10:13 and 2 Samuel 1:18 for biblical references to the Book of Jasher. As for the dating of iron tools, iron ore was smelted and used for iron tools, dating back beyond 3500 B.C., overlapping the Bronze Age. *World Book Encyclopedia,* vol. 2, 10. Chicago: World Book, Inc. 1994.

20 http://c3christiancounseling.com/articles.php The Center for Christian Counseling, Ltd.(469) 635-2200 http://www.rbc.org

21 Elijah House, 317 N. Pines Road, Spokane Valley, Washington, 99206 Phone: (509) 321-1255. www.elijahhouse.org

22 A portion of this research found on the website below. Translation by John Boswell from the Greek *"Passio antiquior SS. Sergii et Bacchi Graece nunc primum edita,"* AB 14 (Brussels, 1895), 373-395.

website: http://www.cs.cmu.edu/afs/cs/user/scotts/ftp/wpaf2mc/serge.html

23 Juster, Dan and Intrater, Keith. *Israel, the Church and the Last Days.* Shippensberg: Destiny Image Publishers, 2003.

24 Roth, Sid. *The Race to Save the World.* Lake Mary, Florida: Charisma House: A Strang Company, 2004. website: www.sidroth.org

25 These literary quotes were heard on a teaching tape by international speaker and author Lance Lambert, who serves as advisor to Christian Friends of Israel-USA. www.cfi-usa.org

26 To order these teachings from worship leader Paul Wilbur, go to www.wilburministries.com "Sixty Minutes with Sid Roth"—"The Best of Paul Wilbur," and "They're Back!"—a teaching on the return of the Sanhedrin after 1700 years and its significance for the Lord's return. Also available are Paul's awesome worship CDs, including "The Watchman," a tremendously anointed worship CD; this music takes us joyfully into the Lord's presence.

27 Bickle, Mike. *The Pleasures of Loving God.* Charisma House: A Strang Company, Lake Mary, FL, 2000.

About the Author

Jill Shannon is a Messianic Jewish Bible teacher, author and singer/song-writer. Growing up in a Reform Jewish home, she accepted the Lord in 1973. In the 1980s, Jill and her husband immigrated to Israel and learned Hebrew, and she gave birth to three children. During these years in Israel, she endured hardship and received vital lessons, shared in this book, "Coffee Talks with Messiah: When Intimacy Meets Revelation."

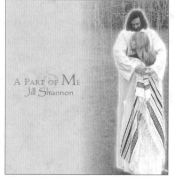

Jill currently speaks and writes about experiencing God's glory, holy living and intimate friendship with the Lord, the biblical Feasts, Israel and the Church. Jill also composes and records worship songs, which can be found on her new CD, "A PART OF ME." She presently resides outside of Philadelphia, Pennsylvania with her husband and two daughters. She also has a married son and daughter-in-law in Pittsburgh, Pennsylvania.

To listen to clips from this intimate worship CD, order CDs, download Jill's free biblical teachings on mp3 files, or to order copies of this book, visit Jill's website:

www.coffeetalkswithMessiah.com

To contact Jill for speaking engagements or book interviews,
e-mail: jill@coffeetalkswithMessiah.com or
jill-shannon@comcast.net or write to:
Coffee Talks
PO Box 26175
Collegeville, PA 19426